THE ROMANS
ON THE
BAY OF NAPLES
AN ARCHAEOLOGICAL GUIDE

THE ROMANS
ON THE
BAY OF NAPLES
AN ARCHAEOLOGICAL GUIDE

LAWRENCE KEPPIE

Photography by Margaret J. Robb

The
History
Press

Photographic images © Margaret J. Robb, except where otherwise credited.

First published 2009

The History Press
The Mill, Brimscombe Port
Stroud, Gloucestershire, GL5 2QG
www.thehistorypress.co.uk

© Lawrence Keppie, 2009

The right of Lawrence Keppie to be identified as the Author
of this work has been asserted in accordance with the
Copyrights, Designs and Patents Act 1988.

British Library Cataloguing in Publication Data.
A catalogue record for this book is available from the British Library.

ISBN 978 0 7524 4840 4

Typesetting and origination by The History Press
Printed in Great Britain

Contents

List of Illustrations

Colour Plates

Acknowledgements

Among the many friends who have aided my researches over the years are Dr
Iain G. Brown and Dr Patricia Andrew, Dr Alison Cooley, Dr Glenys Davies,
Dr Martin Henig, Professor Garrett Fagan, Professor Elizabeth Moignard,
Professor Steven Ostrow, Professor James Russell, Dr Maurizio Simeoni and
Dr Paola Masucci (*Centro Studi Interdisciplinari Gaiola*), Andrea Tramontano
and his colleagues at the Hotel Alpha, Sant'Agnello, Rita Vessichelli Pane at
the Villa Tritone, Sorrento, Terence Volk and Dr Helen Whitehouse.

Former colleagues at the Hunterian Museum and Art Gallery, University
of Glasgow, proved unfailingly helpful. Management and staff at the Grand
Hotel Excelsior Vittoria, Sorrento, allowed access to its grounds, and staff
at the Hotel Bellevue Syrene, Sorrento, to its 'Roman interiors'. Elizabeth
Bell followed up many leads, especially relating to literary travellers
through the centuries. Kay and George Bremner were unstinting in their
offers of hospitality in Oxford, as was Professor Michael H. Crawford
in London. Maria Pia Malvezzi of the British School at Rome valuably
secured permission from the Superintendency of Antiquities for a visit to
the theatre at Herculaneum, and to tombs in the Via dei Cristallini, Naples,
the latter facilitated by Dr Daniela Giampaola. Victoria Brown, curator of
visual resources at the History of Art Department, Oxford, advised on the
photographic firm of Giacomo Brogi and Company.

Professor Alastair Small read a draft version of the complete text, offered
advice based on his long familiarity with the area, and checked details on site.
Dr Iain Brown scrutinised the section on travellers, Dr W.D. Ian Rolfe the
section on geology, and Dr Joanne Berry, Professor Andrew Wallace-Hadrill
and Professor Paul Arthur the accounts of Pompeii, Herculaneum and
Naples respectively, all to my advantage, and responded to specific enquiries.

Margaret Robb was my constant companion on many visits to the area, and took the most of the photographs, except where otherwise credited in the captions. The photograph of the Anglo-American excavation team at Pompeii (*colour plate 24*) is reproduced here by courtesy of Dr Rick Jones, University of Bradford.

The photograph on the front cover, taken from the garden of the Villa Tritone, Sorrento, is reproduced by kind permission of Rita and Mariano Pane. The Villa was constructed *c.*1900 by William Waldorf Astor, who incorporated Roman architectural fragments in its garden. For further information see www.villatritone.it

Line illustrations are by the author; where they have been adapted from published sources, these are acknowledged in the captions.

Introduction

I first visited the Bay and the Roman sites on it in 1970 and have made many subsequent visits, sometimes undertaking research, at other times as the leader of tour groups, or on holiday. One of my earliest memories of it is a day excursion to Pozzuoli in 1971–72, while I was Classical Scholar in the British School at Rome, in the company of John and Margaret Ward-Perkins, Martin Frederiksen and John D'Arms. We went to inspect the newly exposed remains of the temple on the promontory there, not knowing that the structure would subsequently become inaccessible owing to earthquake damage and repeated earth tremors. The late John D'Arms befriended and encouraged me as a young student in Rome and Campania and his book, *Romans on the Bay of Naples* (1970), which described the interrelationships of the many owners of villas on the Bay and visitors to them, including the emperors at Baiae and elsewhere, has remained a particular inspiration. Both Margaret Robb and I briefly participated in excavations at Pompeii undertaken by the British School at Rome and by the University of Bradford.

The present guidebook grew out of a realisation that, while modern tourists are familiar with Pompeii and Herculaneum, they often remain unaware of other, much less crowded attractions. For example, while visitors throng the narrow, stifling streets of Capri in high summer, few take the service bus out of Sorrento the short distance to the Roman villa on Capo di Sorrento, a headland frequented mainly by weekend bathers (below, p. 155).

There is no shortage of books about Pompeii and Herculaneum. The following pages do not seek to emulate their scholarship, but rather to provide an accessible handbook to understanding and appreciating these and many other sites on the ground. No attempt is made here to describe the major archaeological attractions at length, but to advise on how to find and appreciate their 'must see' features. Similarly the reader will find no detailed expositions of the many wall-paintings in individual houses, or of the artworks which adorned them. Space is devoted, often disproportionately, to less visited but still very rewarding sites.

Another hope is that this guidebook will enable readers to view the sites in context, not as islands of archaeology amid modern development and urban sprawl, but as elements in a coherent whole. Monuments belonging to post-Roman times also feature where they may add to the pleasure of a visit. However, I am not dealing, except in passing, with Early Christian basilicas and catacombs, or medieval churches and fortifications along the coast.

In the itineraries below (from p. 53) the modern spellings of place-names are generally given, which are what the traveller needs to look out for, and the Latin forms are used chiefly when specifically referring to the sites in antiquity. It is hoped that not too much confusion will result. The geographical sequence begins with Ischia and Cuma at the north-western end of the Bay, and proceeds in a clockwise direction, ending with Punta della Campanella and the island of Capri at the south-east. The itineraries generally assume that the visitor will be using public transport. The motorcar in other contexts would be the normal mode of travel, but on the Bay roads are crowded, traffic frenetic especially in Naples, and parking at many sites difficult. The area of the Campi Phlegraei (Campi Flegrei), between Miseno and Naples, currently forms the subject of numerous archaeological projects and initiatives, which when brought to fruition will constitute a memorable experience for the visitor lured westwards away from the overcrowded delights of Pompeii and Capri.

The present volume sits in a long line of descriptive guides. Authors range from the Dominican friar Leandro Alberti (1550) and Pompeo Sarnelli, Bishop of Bisceglie (1685), to Augustus Hare (1883). The mid-nineteenth century saw the beginnings of formal guidebooks, published by Karl Baedeker (at Koblenz and, later, Leipzig) and by John Murray (London) for whom Octavian Blewitt wrote the detailed *Handbook for Travellers in Southern Italy* (1853). These, together with S. Russell Forbes' *Rambles in Naples: an archaeological and historical Guide* (London, 1893), remain interesting for descriptions of the remains when the countryside was far less built up, for the bureaucracy associated with travel through the various city-states of Italy before Unification in 1870, the fending off of self-proclaimed guides and 'pretended dealers in antiquities', and modes of transport including carriages, horses, rowing boats, steamers and funicular railways. 'Useful Hints' offered by Forbes included:

> Look sharply after your personal luggage… Pay no attention to touters at the railway… Take lunch in the middle of the day. If you get into a heat, do not go into the shade or into a building till you have cooled down. On inhaling a bad odour, if the stomach is empty, take a nip of brandy, medicinally. Do not over-fatigue yourself.

His advice can surely still be recommended over 100 years later, except perhaps the instruction about the brandy.

Artists were among the visitors attracted to this beautiful coastline: engravings, watercolours and oil paintings offer a closely dated commentary. From the mid-nineteenth century the coastal towns and the landscape were captured in photographs, published for example in the multi-fascicule *Italia Artistica* series (1900 onwards), where we can observe the undeveloped countryside south of Pompeii, lines of changing-cabins for bathers on the beach at Torre Annunziata, the plain of Sorrento where Meta, Piano and Sant' Agnello are isolated hamlets, the comfortable and welcoming spa-town of Castellammare famed for its mineral waters, the single-carriageway autostrada southwards from Naples inaugurated in 1929, Bacoli before any seaside development, Naples before wartime damage and Vesuvius' profile before the 1944 eruption.

The legacy of the eruption of AD 79 manifests itself in plays, operas, cinema epics produced in Hollywood and Cinecittà, and historical novels, notably E.G. Bulwer-Lytton's *The Last Days of Pompeii* (1834) and Robert Harris's *Pompeii* (2003), which presents a wider picture of life on the Bay than the title could suggest. The modern visitor will be confronted by videos, DVDs and increasingly sophisticated and valuably colourful reconstructions on the computer screen. Virtual tours of the major sites can be found on the internet (for Herculaneum, see www.proxima-veritati.auckland.ac.nz). A comprehensive photographic coverage of Pompeii can be found at http://pompeiiinpictures.com. Television re-enactments bring the Roman world before us more dramatically and more accurately than ever before.

The visual appearance both of Pompeii and Herculaneum has been much improved in recent years. Even the numerous dogs lying prostrate on the streets of Pompeii in the summer heat seem less malnourished nowadays.

The major sites are sometimes illuminated at night during festivals and cultural events. In 1997 Pompeii, Herculaneum and Oplontis were jointly 'inscribed' by UNESCO as a World Heritage Site.

However, much remains to be done. The recent government appointment of an 'extraordinary commissioner' for Pompeii promises a welcome enhancement of visitor facilities, including catering outlets and toilets, and the reopening of a number of hitherto closed buildings; visitors will doubtless flood into them. At Herculaneum financial backing from the Packard Humanities Institute (below, p. 98) has enabled much needed conservation to be undertaken, making a considerable difference in a relatively short time.

PART One

Historical and Archaeological Background

1. Geography and Geology

It is hard to avoid Vesuvius. The distinctive profile, changing according to the angle of view, is the Bay's most distinguishing landmark, towering over both the ancient and modern landscape, particularly on a clear day, when a shroud of mist or cloud often crowns the summit (*colour plate 1*); but in the heat haze of summer it can sometimes be all but invisible from a distance. 'Vesuvius is a hellish peak raised up in the midst of paradise', commented Goethe in 1787.

Geologists have long studied the outflows from its many eruptions: the earliest datable was about 25,000 years ago and the most recent was in March 1944 during the Second World War, soon after the Allies had liberated the city of Naples. Lava pouring from its crater swept away buildings in villages high on its slopes, and ash and pumice fell over a wide area, disabling military vehicles and US bombers on an airfield at nearby Terzigno. Some of the volcanic layers now visible originated many centuries after its most famous eruption in AD 79. The latter covered Pompeii, Herculaneum and other sites, preserving them for us but at the cost of many lives. 'Many disasters have befallen the world, but few have brought posterity so much joy', wrote Goethe somewhat unfeelingly after a rewarding visit.

The present-day profile is not the one the Romans would have recognised before AD 79. A wall-painting from the House of the Centenary at Pompeii shows a single lofty peak, thought to represent Vesuvius; but ancient authors imply a flatter surface, perhaps even a crater, which, for example, Spartacus and his followers occupied in 73 BC. The cone that is Vesuvius lies within a larger crater, Monte Somma, which was active until about 15,000 years ago. In antiquity the whole Bay was known colloquially as 'the crater' for its resemblance to a circular wine-mixing bowl, the original meaning of this Greek word.

The landscape of the Bay (*1*) has evolved over the millennia, in part because of the frequent volcanic upheavals, and is in a state of flux even today. Capri was once joined to the mainland, as probably were the islands of Ischia and Procida. Ischia has its own Vesuvius, Monte Epomeo; the mushroom-shaped rock dominating the harbour at Lacco Ameno on Ischia's north coast was ejected from it many thousands of years ago.

It is easy to forget that Vesuvius is not the only volcano on the Bay, just the largest, and certainly not currently the most active. The area west of Naples

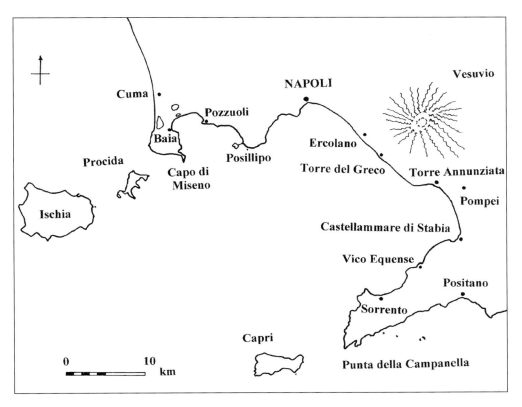

1 The Bay of Naples

was deservedly known, from antiquity, as the Campi Phlegraei or 'Fiery Fields'. One crater occasionally bubbles away – Solfatara near Pozzuoli – and there are others nearby at Astroni, Agnano and Campiglione, as aerial views of the area make immediately clear. Two lakes, Lago d'Averno and Lago di Lucrino, are craters, as are the two adjoining harbours at Miseno. The Bay of Baia is another crater of which one side now lies hidden below the waves. The craggy heights of Posillipo west of Naples constitute part of the rim of a gigantic crater. Several small islands just off the coast are likely volcanic plugs, the remnants of volcanoes now disappeared, including Nisida and the island now occupied by Ischia's castle. At least three craters are identifiable on the islet of Vivara next to Procida. In 1538 a whole new volcano rose up overnight west of Pozzuoli, then as now called Monte Nuovo ('New Mountain').

The Neapolitan royal palace at Portici close to Herculaneum (below, p. 112) was sufficiently near Vesuvius to be at risk from it: the King and his court, on Sir William Hamilton's advice, made a hurried exit at midnight on 19 October 1767, when it was threatened by lava flows. Hester Piozzi (Mrs Thrale), the friend of Dr Samuel Johnson, remarked after a visit in 1784 that if Vesuvius erupted again, the palace at Portici could be buried and future researchers confused between ancient artefacts displayed there and the King's own furniture.

Seismic activity has caused the land west of Naples to rise and fall, a phenomenon generally known as bradyseism. Underwater prospection and aerial photography have revealed the ground-plans of buildings and layouts of streets below the blue waters, especially in the crescent between Baia and Pozzuoli (below, p. 62, 68). Southeast of Naples, lava and falls of ash and pumice have pushed the shoreline out along the coast between Torre del Greco and Castellammare di Stabia.

The constant subterranean activity gave rise to the numerous thermal baths established in ancient, medieval and modern times. Bathing and cure-centres were to be found on Ischia, beside the Lucrine Lake, in the vicinity of Pozzuoli, at Naples, and further round the Bay at Castellammare. Steaming cupolas and sulphuric smells marked out Baiae in Roman times.

Samples of lava, ash and pumice ejected by the volcano were collected by Sir William Hamilton in the eighteenth century, and others can be seen in geological museums in Naples, the modern town of Pompei, at Vico Equense near Sorrento, and worldwide. Hamilton's great work on volcanology, *Campi Phlegraei*, lavishly illustrated with gouaches by Pietro Fabris, was published in Naples in 1776 (*colour plate 2*). Information on excavations at Pompeii, along with engravings by Fabris, was sent by Hamilton to the Society of Antiquaries of London and on volcanic activity to the Royal Society. Hamilton was in the right place at the right time – when Vesuvius was illuminated by day and night, and eruptions were frequent. However, he did not simply report the eruptions but undertook scientific recording of them, in the manner of the Enlightenment scholar. His villa near Portici, equipped with telescopes, served as an observatory and a base for excursions to its slopes (below, p. 48). He devised apparatus, exhibited in London, showing Vesuvius erupting, with accompanying noise and fiery lights.

Nowadays Vesuvius shows little sign of life, and the guides at its crater have to work hard to show tourists some slight escape of steam and smoke (*47*). A more authentic atmosphere may on occasion be experienced near Pozzuoli at the Solfatara, long a clammy, sticky, sulphurous morass (below, p. 78). The spreads of ash and pumice from Vesuvius brought death and destruction, but also fertility to the soil. Vines and olive trees proliferate on its slopes.

In its many eruptions Vesuvius has sometimes poured forth lava which rolled down its slopes, but often ash and pumice have been projected into the sky, raining down on the surrounding country. Earthquakes have shaken, and regularly brought crashing down, surviving Roman, medieval and modern buildings. The zone most affected has regularly lain east and south of Vesuvius, but the effects have been felt over a much wider area. Despite these warnings, the population of the city of Naples has continued to grow. People are loath to abandon family homes and familiar places. When the small town of San Sebastiano al Vesuvio was all but obliterated, not for the first time, in March 1944, its young mayor insisted on reconstruction amid the solidified lava flows which are still very evident there. A National Emergency Plan was formulated in the 1990s and Civil Defence exercises have been held in preparation for a future eruption which all know must come sooner or later. An observatory at Naples monitors seismic activity below Vesuvius with sophisticated electronic equipment.

In the 1970s and 1980s earthquakes did serious damage to Pozzuoli. The historic heart of the town on its promontory jutting out into the Bay was closed off to residents for more than 25 years by concrete barriers set across the access roads. The *Serapeum* at Pozzuoli (below, p. 73) was inundated in the 1970s (*23*), but dried as the ground rose in the 1980s, when the sea retreated from the bustling harbour. In 1980 the Archaeological Museum in Naples and several of the excavated sites were damaged by earth tremors.

The volcanic tuff is easily quarried, as can be seen on many parts of the coastline. Tunnels were dug through it to facilitate travel and communication, several ascribed in antiquity to the engineer Cocceius. Naturally occurring volcanic ash at and near Pozzuoli (hence the modern name Pozzolana), when mixed with lime and in contact with water, could set and remain solid under water.

2. The Eruption of AD 79

In AD 62 or 63 a major earthquake affected several towns on the Bay. We have from the pen of Seneca – by then retired from his post as the young Nero's tutor and enjoying many sojourns in the area – a summary of the damage caused, written shortly after the event. Pompeii had suffered most, but neighbouring towns were affected too, especially Herculaneum, part of which lay in ruins. Many private homes at Neapolis had been destroyed, but no public buildings. Some villas in the countryside had fallen down. There was an impact too, as he reports, on people's confidence in the future. In AD 64 Neapolis was affected by an earthquake which caused the collapse of the theatre, just after Nero had given a performance there (below, p. 91). Other serious tremors of which we have no specific historical record are suspected in the early 70s, all precursors of the cataclysmic events of AD 79; however, when the great eruption came, the populations of the towns below the mountain were unprepared.

The eruption buried Pompeii, Herculaneum, Stabiae and other smaller settlements, so preserving them for us to view and admire, and halting their development with a terrible suddenness. The buried cities did not therefore endure the economic decline and barbarian raids that afflicted the other towns on the Bay in Late Antiquity and after, or acquire new buildings in the Middle Ages, the Renaissance and later centuries to the present day, and they did not suffer from any of the subsequent eruptions. Most ancient towns may have only isolated structures of Roman date, which we can sometimes have difficulty in relating to a town plan, whereas at Pompeii and Herculaneum we can clearly see the close interrelationships of public buildings and domestic spaces.

An account of the events which brought about their destruction in AD 79 was committed to writing many years later by an eyewitness, the then 17-year-old Gaius Plinius Secundus (Pliny the Younger) in two letters (Book vi, 16 and 20) written in AD 106–7 to his friend, the historian Cornelius Tacitus, who was then compiling what would become his *Histories*, covering the period AD 69–96. The relevant chapters of Tacitus' finished work do not survive, so that what he wrote about the AD 79 eruption, doubtless drawing on other primary sources too, is lost to us.

Pliny was at the time staying at Misenum, at the west end of the Bay, perhaps in the 'official residence' of his uncle, also Gaius Plinius Secundus (Pliny the Elder), who held command of the Roman fleet there as its *praefectus*. The letters are of a unique interest in providing a commentary on the archaeology, and vice versa. The modern tourist to the Bay should ideally read them before visiting the ancient sites.

Soon after lunch on the fateful day, people at the Elder Pliny's house became aware that something odd was happening a considerable distance away across the Bay. They climbed upwards to get a better view, and made out a giant mushroom cloud forming in the sky. As they could not see Vesuvius – perhaps as a result of heat haze, mist or cloud – it was only later learned to be the source. The ever studious Younger Pliny preferred to carry on with some piece of work his uncle had given him, but the Elder Pliny, a prominent natural historian, ordered ships to be made ready, and set sail across the Bay for a closer inspection, initially in the hope of rescuing Rectina, a friend who lived directly below the mountain. He was not to know that the natural forces in which he was so interested would be the cause of his own death some 24 hours later. The Elder Pliny could not get ashore as intended, prevented by debris in the sea, and landed further round the Bay at Stabiae (now Castellammare di Stabia) at the villa of a friend, Pomponianus, where he bathed, dined and calmly went to bed. However, when pumice began to fill the courtyard outside his room, he was roused and came out. The group, protecting their heads with pillows against the falling pumice, resolved to descend to the beach, in hope of escape by sea. There Pliny was overcome by gases from the volcano, information which the Younger Pliny gleaned from his uncle's companions during the latter's last moments.

Tacitus subsequently asked for details of the Younger Pliny's own experiences at Misenum, some 30km west of the volcano, and well clear of the worst effects of the eruption. The area nevertheless endured increasingly violent earth tremors throughout the afternoon and evening, then falls of ash during the night, leading to general panic. The Younger Pliny likened the fallen ash to snowdrifts. The people at Misenum – and presumably in other towns towards the west end of the Bay – survived.

The letters themselves do not constitute a comprehensive narrative account of the eruption and its impact. The Younger Pliny had been specifically asked to supply details concerning his uncle's death. Neither Pompeii nor Herculaneum is mentioned by name. From the Younger Pliny's reports and from the geological and archaeological evidence, the eruption in AD 79 was not a single, brief, cataclysmic event: each town was affected in a different way, to different timescales. The volcano began by blasting gritty pumice pebbles (*lapilli*) into the sky, which remained

2 Oplontis, colonnade of the 'Villa of Poppaea', knocked over in AD 79. (L. Keppie)

suspended for several hours, before falling chiefly on and around Pompeii. People there were already fleeing, climbing onto and over, where they could, the increasingly deep layers, with whatever valuables they could carry. Some doubtless took refuge indoors and escaped during lulls; other found themselves entombed.

A gap of some hours was followed by pyroclastic flows and surges: these were hot, fast-moving, ground-hugging clouds of ash and gas, travelling at speeds of 100km per hour or more, which came racing down the slopes, particularly in the direction of Herculaneum. Anyone still alive was asphyxiated instantly, their attitudes and gestures frozen at the moment of death; temperatures reached 400–500 degrees centigrade. People caught in the ashy surges at Pompeii were swiftly enveloped and the body shapes preserved, to be replicated from the later nineteenth century onwards by pumping liquid plaster into the hollows thus formed (below, p. 44). The gritted teeth of some of the victims emphasise the sheer terror of their final moments. At Herculaneum the hot ash-flows stripped flesh from the victims leaving only skeletons, some 300 of which have been located in the years from 1980 onwards below arcadings on the seafront and along the shore (below, p. 98). At Oplontis, the flows and surges were of sufficient force to knock over parts of the villa's porticoes (below, p. 114) on its landward side (*2*). Pliny's account of his uncle's final hours provides a picture of events at Stabiae.

Many people did escape, but any who returned later to search for families or to salvage possessions would find no trace whatever of the town of Herculaneum, buried to a depth of 20–25m (65–80ft). At Pompeii the tops of many buildings, for example the amphitheatre, must still have been recognisable, but most of the town lay under a blanket up to 5m (16ft) deep. Archaeological exploration has revealed shafts and tunnels, some at least of which testify to attempts, probably successful if good landmarks were available, to locate individual houses. The coverage at Stabiae was much less deep, but the seafront villas there were not cleared for re-occupation. The modern visitor can still see material expelled from the volcano in AD 79 at, for example, Oplontis, Boscoreale, outside the Nuceria Gate at Pompeii, and beside the House of Argus in Herculaneum.

The emperor Titus in Rome, who had succeeded his father Vespasian only a few months earlier, visited the area and established a commission of ex-consuls who redistributed the property of those who had died without heirs. Casualties individually mentioned in the literary sources included an otherwise barely known poet Caesius Bassus, believed incinerated in his villa on the slopes of Vesuvius, and a grandson of King Herod Agrippa of Judaea. Nothing was done to re-establish Pompeii or Herculaneum, which had been effectively erased from the map. Public buildings in neighbouring towns were repaired as necessary, their territories extended, the land freshly surveyed and re-allocated, and the road network was re-established. Life resumed. The memory of the existence of Pompeii, Herculaneum and other places was retained during Roman times, and later became the stuff of legend. Scholars in Renaissance times and later knew of their existence from surviving literary works and from inscriptions, but the main sites were not conclusively located again until the eighteenth century (below, p. 43).

The events of AD 79 can be studied on the basis of different bodies of evidence: literary (principally Pliny's letters to Tacitus), archaeological (the sites themselves and the finds made there) and geological (samples taken on and around the volcano). The geological and the archaeological evidence indicates that the areas affected were to the south and east, reaching to the Sorrentine peninsula, Capri, the Amalfi coast, and the Gulf of Salerno to Paestum and beyond. However, dark clouds of ashy material, we are told, were observed in the sky at Rome, in North Africa, Syria and Egypt.

The psychological effects on the survivors must have been severe for the next half century. Whole families perished in the space of little more than a day. The profile of the mountain itself was permanently altered. The ash which we are told by the Younger Pliny fell on Misenum was doubtless swept up and carted off. The extensive photographic and cinefilm record of the eruption of March 1944, some now available online, deepens our awareness of the catastrophe.

In recent years there has been a spirited debate on a matter we have long taken for granted: the time of year in AD 79 when Vesuvius erupted. Modern translations of Pliny's letters offer a specific day, 24 August, or in Roman terms, 'the ninth day before the Kalends [the first day] of September', relying on the text of some but by no means all of the surviving manuscripts of Pliny's *Letters*. However, a number of Italian archaeologists have over many years expressed reservations about the August dating. The matter was already in dispute before the end of the nineteenth century. Advocates of a date later in AD 79, the ninth day before the Kalends of December [that is 23 November, a shorter month than August], have pointed to the presence of braziers in some houses, warmly clad bodies of victims, and botanical evidence in the form of fruit, seeds and pips. A coin hoard found in the House of the Golden Bracelet at Pompeii includes a silver *denarius* issued after September AD 79 but before January 80. Attention has also been drawn, less convincingly, to the sequence of events in Cassius Dio's much later *History* of the period, in which intimation of Julius Agricola's successes as governor in Britain, during the late summer of AD 79, reached Rome *before* news of the eruption in Campania, an event which Dio places 'at the close of autumn'.

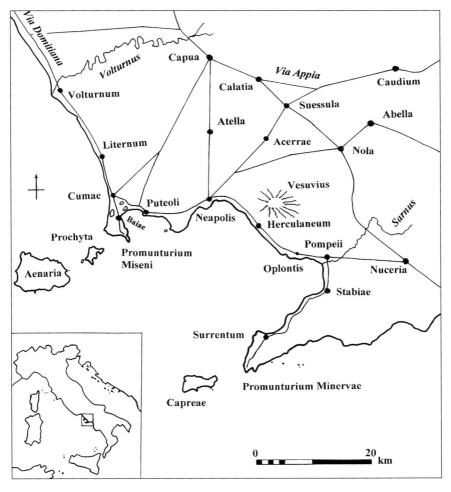

3 Campania and the Bay of Naples in Roman times. (After Ward–Perkins and Claridge 1976)

3. Roman Conquest and Settlement

Several hundred years were to pass between the foundation of the little town on the Tiber in 753 BC and the spread of its power and influence to the area around the Bay. It was not an empty land. Earlier human habitation in the region the Romans called Campania ('the flat country') and along the coast is evidenced by archaeological finds of prehistoric tools in stone and metal and of settlement sites. Already by the time of the legendary Trojan War in the thirteenth century BC, Mycenaeans from mainland Greece were trading with Sicily and Southern Italy, and have left traces of their activities in the form of trade goods on Ischia and nearby Procida.

Colonisation from Greece and from existing Greek colonies in Sicily began in the mid-eighth century BC, with trading settlements first on Ischia and Procida, and then on the mainland at Cuma, an important centre from which daughter settlements were established at Dicaiarchia (Pozzuoli), Naples, Herculaneum and other locations.

Another external force was the Etruscans who had expanded south from their homeland north of the Tiber by the seventh century BC; their settlements round the Bay included Pompeii. These Greek and Etruscan coastal towns became locked in conflict for mastery of the land with the indigenous tribes of southern Italy, especially the Samnites, and had been ground by them into submission a century before the Romans appeared on the scene.

The earliest phase of formal Roman settlement belongs in the third century BC, by which time a wide swathe of territory north and east of the Bay was already subject to Rome. In 273 a colony was established at Paestum on the Gulf of Salerno. Colonies in the ancient world were essentially small agricultural settlements, with a town-site often built from scratch as a marketplace and the centre of local government. At other times existing townships were subordinated to the new masters, as was the case at Paestum, which had flourished as the Greek colony of Poseidonia (named for the sea-god Poseidon), to whose sixth and fifth century BC heyday belong the construction of the three magnificent temples which still stand there. Paestum was not a 'Roman' colony in that the settlers were specifically of Roman stock, but 'Latin' (a secondary status, named for Latium, modern Lazio, the 'broad lands' around the Tiber mouth).

After long years of war in the final decades of the third century BC, which saw the eventual defeat of Hannibal in 201, colonies of Roman citizens (as opposed to Latins) were established in 194 at Volturnum (Castelvolturno) and Liternum (at Lago di Patria) on the coast north of Cumae, on the Bay at Puteoli (Pozzuoli), and further south at Salernum (Salerno). These were as much garrison outposts as agricultural settlements, and were linked to Rome by an ever-expanding road system. Other towns – including Pompeii and Herculaneum – remained 'allied', with no rights associated with citizenship, whether the latter was the coveted 'Roman' or the less privileged 'Latin'. In 90–89 BC a large number of these allied towns, including Pompeii, rose in revolt, in the so-called Social War and, after a hard struggle and significant concessions by Rome, 'allied' and 'Latin' status in peninsular Italy was swept away; all freeborn men and women living south of the River Po became full Roman citizens.

The following decades were to witness a series of civil wars, as politicians and generals vied for supremacy. This was the time of Lucullus, Pompey, Cicero, Caesar, Brutus and Mark Antony, one of the best documented periods of Roman history. The rich literary sources highlight the ever increasing popularity of the Bay as a destination for wealthy Romans who purchased or constructed villas on the coast. Many of these owners were individually buffeted by wider political events, in which they lost their properties and sometimes their lives.

Inland, the lulls between bouts of civil war saw the establishment or reinforcement of colonies, now principally rewarding time-served soldiers of the victorious protagonists with sizeable plots of agricultural land, settlements which often overflowed into the territories of adjacent towns. This represented a major transplantation of population and a mixing of local cultures, as the legions were made up of men from a wide variety of backgrounds who found themselves transported en masse, without any choice of location, to unfamiliar regions of Italy. Many would bring wives, families or parents to start a new life as farmers. Officers such as tribunes and centurions became natural leaders in their new civilian life. Existing landholders were dispossessed, sometimes with offers of land elsewhere. Puteoli was a colony of this type, as was Nuceria inland from Pompeii, but the other communities on the coast remained relatively untouched.

These catastrophic events ushered in the strong rule of one man, Octavian, Caesar's great-nephew and adopted son, who in 27 BC took the prestigious title Augustus, and is recognised as the first Roman emperor. His long reign through to AD 14 allowed the new system to bed in. Augustus himself acquired, or had inherited, several properties on the Bay. In 29 BC he arranged for the town of Neapolis (Naples) to transfer to his ownership the island of Capreae (Capri), giving it the island of Aenaria (Ischia) in exchange, and developed it as a private preserve (below, p. 160). Recalcitrant or dynastically awkward younger members of the imperial family were sometimes exiled by Augustus and his successors to isolated offshore islands, including Pontia (Ponza) and Pandateria (Ventotene) some distance west of the Campanian mainland. Traditionally seen as imprisoned on 'desert islands', they in fact enjoyed the use of elaborate villas, which archaeology has revealed.

Under Augustus a naval base was established on the Bay, developed by his chief lieutenant, the resourceful Agrippa, firstly at the Lucrine Lake near Baiae, and subsequently at Misenum, at the north-western end of the Bay, which sprouted on-shore facilities for a fleet of several hundred ships.

Augustus' successor Tiberius lived on Capri for much of the last 11 years of his rule (AD 26–37), from which he directed the affairs of empire. Tiberius' successors kept ownership of the island, but also favoured other locations on the Bay such as Baiae. Emperor Caligula, to impress Parthian royal hostages (and to refute a prophesy), had a bridge of boats constructed from Bauli, just south of Baiae, to Puteoli, and rode across it in both directions, on horseback and then in a chariot, followed by some of the Praetorian Guard. It was from Baiae that the emperor Nero, after entertaining his mother Agrippina to supper in March AD 59, sent her homewards to nearby Bauli in a collapsible boat. She escaped from the poorly designed craft when it failed to capsize properly, despite the best efforts of the complicit crew, and swam ashore, only to be killed shortly afterwards by sailors sent from Misenum. The imperial presence on the Bay, though maintained thereafter, largely fades from our written record: the emperors needed to spend more time in the provinces, on or near the Empire's frontiers.

4. Town and Country

Like any other part of Italy, the Bay of Naples was a patchwork of communities, each with a town as the market centre surrounded by an often extensive territory. The precise boundaries are not always to be determined, even after centuries of research and scholarship. However, the names and the locations of the towns are not in doubt (3): in sequence from north-west to south-east they were Cumae (Cuma), Misenum (Miseno), Puteoli (Pozzuoli), Neapolis (Naples), Herculaneum (Ercolano), Pompeii (Pompei), Stabiae (Castellammare di Stabia) and Surrentum (Sorrento). Inland there were, among many others, Capua (Santa Maria Capua Vetere) and Nuceria (Nocera), and further south, beyond the confines of the Bay, Salernum (Salerno) and Paestum.

A town's wealthiest families provided its magistrates, who were elected to local office on an annual basis. In a colony such as Pompeii, the *Duoviri* were its two chief magistrates with judicial functions. Two *Aediles* superintended markets and kept the streets clean. In towns lacking colonial status — such as Herculaneum and Surrentum — these four office-holders were often grouped together as *Quattuorviri*. A town's finances were overseen by two *Quaestores*. A hundred-strong town council, the *Ordo* of Decurions, consisting for the most part of ex-magistrates, acted as a check on the current officeholders and provided continuity. We know the names of many magistrates at Pompeii under the Early Empire and can often gauge from decade to decade which families were up, which down. From the survival of election notices there, painted on external house-walls along the main thoroughfares (*colour plate 16*), the names of some candidates for election in AD 79 are known, but not who were elected that year, or whether they survived the eruption barely a few months into their year of office, which in Roman towns began on 1 July. Such notices are much rarer at Herculaneum.

For the Romans, the most important town on the Bay was not Neapolis, and certainly not Pompeii, but Puteoli which developed into one of Italy's leading ports, at which the annual corn fleets from Egypt landed their contents, to feed, in later conjunction with Ostia at the Tiber mouth, the ever-growing population of Rome. In Roman times the Bay was generally known as the *sinus Puteolanus*, the Gulf of Puteoli.

The road system in Italy had its origins in a need for Rome to maintain good communication with its colonies, in areas ever more remote from the mother city. The chief highway south from Rome was the *Via Appia* (Appian Way), established in the late fourth century BC, which headed first to Capua, the leading inland city of the flat country of Campania. From Capua roads led to the Bay, as well as south-east, in a continuation of the *Via Appia*, eventually to Brundisium (Brindisi), from which travellers embarked for the sea crossing to Greece. Another road, later upgraded as the *Via Domitiana* (Domitianic Way), followed the west coast of Italy southwards from Sinuessa (Mondragone) to Puteoli.

Many lesser roads linked the individual seaside communities. Under the Empire most roads were paved with stone and the inequalities evened out by gravel, though their construction had been much simpler in earlier centuries. The modern visitor will soon become familiar with the streets of Pompeii and Herculaneum, evocatively but unevenly paved with volcanic stone, with high pavements on either side (*4*). At Pompeii regularly-set sequences of stepping stones facilitated crossing of the streets, useful if rainwater was running down them, but at Herculaneum there were underground sewers into which the water could drain. Ruts worn in some of the paving at Pompeii show the volume of wheeled traffic

4 Pompeii, stepping stones at the junction between the Via dell'Abbondanza and the Via Stabiana

and the width of axles. There must surely have been a network of one-way streets; recent research has identified traffic flows at Pompeii, regulated by bollards.

The ancient traveller on a Roman road through the countryside would see laden donkeys, wagons and carriages with two or four wheels drawn by mules, and litters carried by slaves, though not chariots which – despite the best efforts of Hollywood to implant them in our minds as a feature of Roman daily life – were already museum-pieces. The traveller could gauge distances along a road by pausing at the cylindrical milestones erected every 1000 paces, inscribed with the names of Roman magistrates or later the emperor who had overseen the construction of, or financed, the road, with the distance from Rome (or a major town) marked on them. Milestones are on view at some of the museums round the Bay. The traveller would pass scattered farmhouses, roadside posting stations and inns, occasional family tombs and of course aqueducts, whether raised on arches or set in underground channels. The Aqua Augusta, built under Augustus, brought water from the hills at Serino near Avellino to all the major towns on the Bay by a series of branch-channels. The aqueduct's general course is securely known, but there is little of it for the modern visitor to see, except in Naples (below, p. 93) or by carefully searching it out.

A great many farmhouses (*villae rusticae*) have been located and several excavated, especially in the countryside north and east of Pompeii and inland from Castellammare. One has been reconstructed at Boscoreale (below, p. 118; *colour plate 12*). Some are likely to have been owned by leading town-based families; a few were in imperial ownership. Some may have been originally built by colonists established at Pompeii in the early first century BC. Most were productive farms serving the adjacent towns and many had been extended to allow for more gracious living. There has been little excavation of such farmsteads in modern times anywhere west of Naples, except on the outskirts of Pozzuoli, and we often lack comprehensible ground plans. Part of a *villa rustica* of early imperial date has been opened up on Capri, at Gasto close to the Marina Grande.

Not all travel was by land. Ferries operated along the coasts from the Tiber to the Bay. The rich arrived at their coastal villas in their own craft, either direct from Rome or by embarking further round the Bay. Oared warships would be seen entering or exiting the naval base at Misenum, and convoys of cornships heading for Puteoli; the presence of a naval base and the economic importance of the food supply were interconnected.

Commercial shipping, transporting for example exotic animals from Africa to the amphitheatres of Italy and especially Rome, also docked at Puteoli.

5. Life and Society

We are excellently placed to reconstruct a picture of Roman life on this favoured coastline of Italy, from a rich combination of literary, epigraphic and archaeological sources. Pompeii and Herculaneum were towns of middling importance: the former had perhaps 12,000 inhabitants, and the latter about 4000–5000. The normal daily round of activities was no different to other towns. For us it is their unforeseen destruction in a matter of 36 hours which draws our attention; many of the inhabitants were dead, the rest homeless refugees.

This was a slave-run economy, where farms, town houses and luxury villas depended on the labour of the slaves who worked the fields or acted as servants. A slave could be freed by his master for good service or in his will, which allowed the newly freed man and his family to begin to rise in society. The freedmen themselves often became shopkeepers or small businessmen, sometimes in association with their former masters, and the particularly successful could show off their wealth as *Augustales*, an organisation centred on loyalty to the imperial family and whose members were, less certainly, active priests of the cult of the emperors (below, p. 60). Children of freedmen were full Roman citizens and males could run for municipal office in the normal way.

Some picture of this world comes from the *Satyricon*, a novel ascribed to Petronius, a senator prominent under Nero. Its best known episode is the 'Banquet of Trimalchio', which scholars believe is loosely set in the commercial world of rich freedmen at Puteoli, the great port town. Petronius offers a picture, comic and sometimes grotesque, of the lifestyles of some of the Bay's most upwardly mobile and successful entrepreneurs.

Those who thronged the streets of towns on the Bay were astonishingly multicultural for those of us who might think they were all 'Romans'. Some were Roman citizens; others were freeborn men and women from the Empire's provinces, and others were freedmen. Many were slaves acquired from recently conquered provinces, or the descendants of them.

Thanks to the survival of graffiti and painted notices on walls, a wide cross-section of the population of Pompeii (and, to a lesser extent, Herculaneum) comes before us (*colour plate 16*). People scratched words and phrases on any available surface, sometimes none too politely, identifying their occupations and crucially their preoccupations. Wax writing-tablets from Pompeii and nearby Moregine (below, p. 145) reveal the details of complex business transactions.

These were self-governing townships, equipped with public buildings for administration, entertainment, recreation, and religious observance. The grandest buildings in any town were an amphitheatre for gladiatorial contests and wild-beast hunts, one or more theatres, and sometimes a circus for chariot-racing or a stadium for athletics (on the Bay only at Puteoli, and perhaps Neapolis). There would also be an open-air *palaestra* for exercise.

The political and social centre of any Roman town was its Forum, along whose sides temples, lawcourts, market halls and administrative buildings were erected. Each town had a number of public baths (*thermae*), with rooms heated to varying temperatures by furnaces or supplied by naturally hot springs. Baths were a social meeting place, where the bather, accompanied by his or her slaves, went from room to room, in a ritual which might last several hours. There were usually separate rooms for men and women. Clothes were left in the *apodyterium* (undressing room), and the bather went first to the *frigidarium* (cold room). Next he or she proceeded to the *tepidarium* (warm room), and finally to the *caldarium* (hot room), subsequently retracing their steps to the *frigidarium* where a dip in a cold plunge bath closed up the pores, before exiting into the street.

The philosopher Seneca, writing in the early 60s AD, gives us a valuable account.

I'm living above baths. Picture to yourself all varieties of sound ... Macho types for example are exercising with leaden weights in their hands; when they are working hard, or at least pretending to, I hear the groans ... Perhaps I fall in with some passive fellow, content with a cheap rub-down, and hear the crack a hand makes on his shoulders ... Add now the arresting of a brawler or petty thief, and the man who likes to hear the sound of his own voice at the baths, or those who jump into the swimming tank with a huge splash ... The hair-plucker with his penetrating, shrill voice .... Next the distinctive shoutings of the pastry-seller, the sausage-man, the confectioner.

Seneca does not specify the location of these particular baths, though the description is generally attributed to one of the towns on the Bay.

The practice of religion in Roman times centred on temples and shrines, the former large and very imposing, the latter sometimes quite small and temporary. Like many of the public buildings in a town, temples were often constructed at the expense of individuals. Pompeii and other colonies had a *Capitolium*, dedicated jointly to the triad of Jupiter, Juno and Minerva, in imitation of the Temple of Jupiter on the Capitoline Hill at Rome.

5 Pompeii, altar in front of the 'Temple of Vespasian', showing the sacrifice of a bull. (L. Keppie)

Roman temples were generally, unlike their Greek predecessors, raised on a substantial podium, and open only at the front through a colonnaded porch. The statue of the deity was out of sight inside, and the priests, normally drawn from a town's richest families, conducted ceremonies and sacrifices on an outdoor altar at the foot of the temple steps (5). Towns rarely possessed a temple to every deity. The public worship of the living emperor was already gaining ground under Augustus, and it soon became normal to venerate each emperor in turn and sometimes dead emperors who had been designated *divus*. Exotic cults encountered by the Romans in their conquest of lands round the eastern Mediterranean or spread by travellers included Mithras, the Persian god of truth and light, Isis, the Egyptian goddess of fertility and childbirth, Serapis, the multi-faceted Egyptian god of the underworld, and Cybele, the Anatolian mother-goddess. These cults generally offered the worshipper a greater opportunity of personal involvement.

However, the greatest proportion of space in any town was occupied by private housing. The houses uncovered at Pompeii and Herculaneum have long conditioned our assessment of domestic buildings throughout the Roman world; there were numerous variations in plan, the result of extensions, amalgamations, the varying dimensions of the plot available, and personal preferences of the owners. Typically the visitor entered from the street through a narrow corridor, arriving first at the *atrium* (6) with its central cistern for rainwater (the *impluvium*), beyond which was usually a reception room (*tablinum*), where the owner might await him.

Often the house was guarded by a ferocious dog chained up inside the entrance. The *cave canem* ('beware of the dog') mosaic at the House of the Tragic Poet is one of Pompeii's most reproduced images (7). A small domestic shrine (a *lararium*) at or near the *atrium* served for the family's sacrifices to the spirits protecting the household (8). When found, some *lararia* were still equipped with statuettes placed by the family. Houses had few windows onto the street, and might be shielded from noise and bustle by shops, sometimes leased out to the family's own freedmen. Beyond or adjacent to the reception room were bedrooms and at least one formal dining room (*triclinium*), named for the triple couches facing inwards towards the dinner table. Meals would be taken outdoors in the summer. Internal walls were decorated with wall-paintings and their floors with mosaics, according to prevailing styles and the financial capacity of the owner (below p. 47). Scenes from Graeco-Roman mythology were especially popular subjects

6 Pompeii, colonnaded *atrium* of the House of M. Epidius Rufus, on the north side of the
Via dell'Abbondanza

for wall-paintings, as were views of the countryside, with plants, birds and
fountains.

The basic house-plan centred on the *atrium* was soon augmented by an
enclosed garden framed by a peristyle, and ornamented with fountains
and sculpture in stone and bronze. Many gardens have been investigated
archaeologically by the late Professor Wilhelmina Jashemski, to reveal
hedging, shrubbery and vegetable plots (*9*). In the south-eastern quadrant
of Pompeii garden spaces were extensively planted with vines and olive
trees.

Petronius in his *Satyricon* provides a picture – exaggerated certainly
and full of comic scenes, but presumably immediately recognisable to his
readers – of the routine of Trimalchio's household on an evening when the

7 Pompeii, *cave canem* mosaic at the entrance to the House of the Tragic Poet. (L. Keppie)

owner was entertaining, and the economics of supplying it. When the chief characters arrived for dinner, one was startled by the painted image of a dog near the door, believing it real. The enormous snarling dog itself, Scylax, a name which ironically means 'pup', was subsequently introduced to the diners, and later, when they were leaving the banquet somewhat inebriated, one of them was so startled by the dog's barking that he fell into a fishpond; their attendant used the contents of a food bag to distract it.

Outside the walls of a Roman town, cemeteries stretched along the roads leading into the countryside. We know most about those at Pompeii and, increasingly, at Puteoli. Similar cemeteries doubtless stretched away from the gates at Herculaneum and other towns, but we are less able to document them. Cremation was the normal procedure, with the ashes placed in a small

stone ash-chest or in a glass or ceramic jar. In some tombs – such as the communal house-shaped *columbaria* (literally 'dovecotes') – the containers lay in a niche, sealed by an inscribed stone plaque. The richest families erected elaborate tomb structures, sometimes in the form of temples (*10*) or large altars, conspicuously sited for the passer-by to admire. Seating enticed the weary traveller approaching the town's gates, to rest and read the name and civic distinctions of the deceased.

Opposite top:
8 Pompeii, *lararium* in the House of the Vettii. (L. Keppie)

Opposite bottom:
9 Pompeii, peristyle of the House of Venus in a Shell, on the Via dell'Abbondanza

Right: 10 Pompeii, tomb of M. Octavius and his wife Vertia Philumina, outside the Nuceria Gate

6. Villas on the Coast

Just as the modern coast of the Bay nowadays attracts both permanent residents and short-term holidaymakers, so too in antiquity. The geographer Strabo, writing during the reign of Augustus, observed that the coastline between Misenum and Surrentum resembled a continuous city; such was the preponderance of large houses and cultivated woodland.

The great aristocrats owned villas by the sea (*villae maritimae*), some of which the emperors acquired by inheritance, confiscation or purchase, and which they elaborated or extended. Cicero, Seneca, Statius and Philostratus all offer descriptions of coastal villas, accounts which can occasionally be linked to actual remains. The Elder Pliny spent his last few remaining hours of life at a villa in Stabiae, which had baths, a dining room and a courtyard leading to the apartment turned over to him, with the beach in front. We can readily envisage its overall layout (below, p. 146).

The oppressive heat of Rome in the summer months drove the rich to the nearby Sabine Hills or Alban Hills, and to the coast. Wealthy families had a multiplicity of properties in the most desirable localities, which their freedmen and slaves maintained in the owners' frequent absences. We need not think in terms of just one 'second home'. The Late Republic witnessed a frenetic buying up of properties and land along the coast, and either the enlargement of existing farmhouses or the construction of completely new houses. Other owners were the prominent families or *nouveaux riches* of the nearby towns. The emperor's occasional presence on the Bay meant that detachments of his household troops, the Praetorian Guard, were in attendance.

Some of these maritime villas, with their terraces, baths, gardens, and porticoes descending to the shore, covered immense areas, adapting the local topography to their owner's whims. The staff-intensive villas on the coast might be financially supported by inland properties, whose surplus produce supplied their needs. The poet Martial, writing at the end of the first century AD, mentions a villa at Baiae of a friend Faustinus, which was atypically not laid out with unprofitable expanses of myrtles, planes and boxwood hedges, but given over to cornfields and vineyards, with cattle, sheep, pigs and poultry, to serve nearby markets. Ancient authors emphasise the importance of fishponds and semi-submerged tanks for fish-farming offshore. Fish were sometimes kept as pets, and owners went to extraordinary lengths to cosset them.

We must not think of these coastal villas as widely spaced, with extensive grounds and formal driveways. They might be closely set as at Baiae and

Stabiae. Owners gloried in their ostentatious properties and in the artworks with which they filled them. Catching up on reading in one's own library or those of neighbours and friends was a favourite occupation. The majority of luxury villas which Roman owners built on the Bay were positioned directly on the coast, availing themselves of spectacular seaward views. Some combined a sea view with proximity to a town (the so-called *villae suburbanae*), like the Villa of the Mysteries at Pompeii and the splendid Villa of the Papyri just outside Herculaneum.

Wall-paintings from Pompeii and Stabiae depict the general types of villas and perhaps on occasion specific sites with pools, fountains, arcades and jetties. Some villas were extended over the sea, supported on concrete piles, or incorporated natural springs; such constructions involved stupendous feats of engineering, aided by the *pozzolana* concrete. Terraces extended along the cliffs, with arcading to support a level platform, just as in more modern times at, for example, the monastery of Camaldoli della Torre (high above the A3 Autostrada near Torre del Greco) and at the eighteenth and nineteenth century seafront villas at Sorrento and Sant'Agnello.

So much attention has been paid to the pre-eruption landscape that it is easy to forget that in places villa-owning continued, sometimes atop the ash, pumice and mud after AD 79. Soon however many of the Empire's richest men came from the Roman provinces, and their principal landholdings lay outside Italy.

7. Archaeology of the Sites

For us it is now difficult to appreciate that the precise whereabouts of Pompeii and Herculaneum were long unknown. Scholars had argued for this location or that, but it was only in the eighteenth century that the sites of both towns were conclusively identified. The Bourbon kings of Naples were at the forefront of excavation of the known sites, and the searching out of new ones, principally to obtain sculpture, wall-paintings, mosaics and objets d'art. Small archaeological finds such as pottery, lamps and coins, where they were kept at all, were carried off to their palaces at Portici or Naples, without adequate record of their provenance. Excavation was controlled subsequently by the Italian State, under successive superintendents, of whom the best known are Giuseppe Fiorelli (in post 1863–75) and Amadeo Maiuri (1924–62). Teams from many European countries, America and Japan have worked at the major sites. Some recent excavations at Pompeii are on a very large scale, involving dozens of workmen, students and volunteers (*colour plate 24*). Others have followed the lines of services in modern towns, or been undertaken below piazzas in Naples (below, p. 87).

The archaeological sites themselves were covered later by lava flows, pumice and ash falls in medieval times, and shaken sometimes irreparably by earthquakes, damaged by wartime bombing in 1943, in more recent decades collapsing through sheer debility and the effects of rain and sun. In 2006 when excavators at the Temple of Venus at Pompeii unearthed the casing of a Second World War star-shell, part of the main site was closed off until it was confirmed as harmless.

The process of uncovering the sites continues, but about 40 per cent of Pompeii remains unexplored beneath farmers' smallholdings, and an unknown percentage of Herculaneum lies deep beneath solidified volcanic material, in part overtopped by modern housing. The visitor to either site will quickly notice the constant battle to maintain and secure the remains presently visible, without further work adding to commitments and costs for future generations. The restoration of buildings to roof height has involved the re-erecting of columns, reconstruction of upper walls, and the replacing of tiled roofs. Many buildings were much more closed-in than we see them nowadays.

A frequent feature of many books and television documentaries on Pompeii is an emphasis on the large number of bodies of its inhabitants who were unable to escape the volcano's ire in AD 79. Numerous skeletons were found in the early excavations, but in 1863 Giuseppe Fiorelli experimented with pouring plaster into cavities in the solidified ashy deposits which were then removed to reveal body-shapes and even facial expressions (*11*). At Pompeii many bodies were found well above street level, not in the initial pumice falls but entombed in the overlying ash. A fleeing group heading for the open countryside, carrying jewellery, their house keys, lamps to light the way in the darkness and purses full of money, passed through the Nola Gate on the town's north-east side, but succumbed on the roadway outside. Members of a family, including a pregnant woman, were found together in a room at the back of the House of Julius Polybius. The casts show vividly that death was far from painless. A few bodies wearing ankle-shackles were presumably slaves. The body-shapes of farm and domestic animals have also been cast in this way, as have wooden doors and shuttering.

11 Pompeii, plaster cast of a hunched-up male, who is protecting his nose and mouth with his hands

Far fewer human remains have been found over the years at Herculaneum, though mention can be made of the skeleton of a baby in its wood-framed rocking cot found in the House of M. Pilius Primigenius above the Suburban Baths. However, from 1980 onwards several hundred skeletons were found in hitherto unexcavated arcadings on the seafront and on the adjacent shore. The villas at Stabiae and Oplontis have also yielded skeletal remains. Such skeletons are particularly valuable to modern biologists, since at this time most Romans were cremated; examination of the bones allows study of height, age-range, diseases and genetic make-up. Analysis of human sewage at Herculaneum has provided details of diet and the meals eaten in the days preceding the eruption.

The unearthing of Pompeii and Herculaneum from the eighteenth century onwards provided contemporaries and their descendents to the present day with a vivid and unrivalled picture of life in Roman towns, not just the streets, houses, public buildings, fountains and statues, interior decoration and furniture in wood and metal, but material culture in the form of kitchen utensils, jewellery, crockery in bronze, and coins in their pockets or purses. Gold and silver tableware has been recovered in towns and at country villas, not always from luxurious properties. Modern visitors should look out for the details of daily life, so like our own.

Archaeologists are normally reliant on their estimation of standing remains, or the assemblage of small finds recovered during an excavation or otherwise associated with a site, for their conclusions about its date and the length of occupation and use. However, any student of the Roman remains from Pompeii, Herculaneum and other settlements in the vicinity of Vesuvius has a unique advantage in that everything found there was in use in AD 79, and not thereafter. This *terminus ante quem* has greatly aided the study of building styles and assemblages elsewhere in Italy and more widely throughout the Roman Empire.

In towns not buried by the eruption, there is no such fixed cut-off point: buildings continued in use and to be built or rebuilt into Late Antiquity and the Middle Ages, for example in Naples and Pozzuoli where modern observers must depend for dating on an assessment of the stone, brick-faced or bare concrete structures confronting them. The continued use of some buildings – such as the baths at Baiae – into the Middle Ages and beyond helps to account for the exceptional degree of preservation. Finds too have been made by underwater investigation below the waters of the Bay, and wrecks pinpointed, for example recently off Capri. Further such discoveries can be expected.

As in any town down to modern times, not all the buildings now visible in Pompeii and Herculaneum had been recently put up; what we see reflects generations of alteration, adjustment and redecoration. Where repairs were in hand in the aftermath of the earthquake of AD 62–3, the building work must date to within a decade and a half of the eruption. In some cases such work was actually in progress when disaster struck. The earliest surviving houses at Pompeii were of squared stone blocks (*opus quadratum*) of the local limestone or volcanic tuff. With the invention of concrete, ever more elaborate and substantial structures were possible, including arches, vaulting and domes, for example at Baiae. From the late third century BC onward it became normal to face a concrete core with stone, at first in an irregular pattern (*opus incertum*), then from the mid-first century BC in a regular diamond pattern (*opus reticulatum*). Brick-faced concrete (*opus latericium*) began to be used in the early to mid-first century BC, and can be seen too in repairs to earlier structures. The most popular form of construction in the aftermath of the AD 62–3 earthquake at Pompeii was *opus vittatum mixtum*, which involved horizontal courses of bricks alternating with those of squared stones (*80*). In antiquity such facings were not, with a few exceptions, meant to be seen: the walls were plastered and some coated in red paint. It is only because the plaster covering was washed away, or has collapsed, that we see the structure behind.

Internally, the walls of houses and of public buildings were decorated, almost without exception, with painted scenes, which are divided chronologically into four main 'styles', beginning in the mid-second century BC and ending in AD 79. This was fresco-painting, where paint was applied to plaster which was not yet dry, sometimes on incised guidelines. The First Style (*c.*150–90 BC) used simple coloured panels imitating stone blocks, framed by raised stucco borders. The Second Style (*c.*90–25 BC) employed large pictorial scenes within elaborate architectural frameworks. The Third Style (*c.*25 BC–*c.*AD 40) concentrated on smaller vignettes with less illusionist facades; and the Fourth Style (*c.*AD 40–79 at Pompeii and Herculaneum, and elsewhere up to AD 100) combined several traits of the Second and Third Styles.

Floors were commonly of waterproof concrete mixed with tile or lava fragments (generally termed *opus signinum*). More expensive was *opus sectile*, a smooth surface of cut marble in geometric forms. Wealthier families could afford mosaics, made up from small cube-shaped *tesserae* of coloured stones or glass paste.

8. Travellers and Tourists

The modern tourist stands in a long line of visitors. In Roman times the Bay attracted travellers from the many provinces of the Roman Empire. In the Middle Ages they included Dante (1265–1321), Petrarch (1304–74) and Boccaccio (1312–75). Several visitors from England in the sixteenth and seventeenth centuries have left a written record of their experiences (see Bibliography). From about 1700 the area attracted swarms of young aristocratic visitors who travelled, often with their tutors, from Britain, France or the German states on a comprehensive tour which might take in Venice, Florence, Rome and Naples. Some ventured further south to

Paestum, or even Sicily. Greece at this time was not readily accessible and its wonders were often known only through classical texts. The eruptions of Vesuvius were an unfailing fillip to tourist numbers, with people travelling south from Rome or much further afield to witness its activities.

The revealing of parts of Pompeii and Herculaneum in the eighteenth century did not establish Naples as a tourist destination but merely reinforced it. For earlier travellers the area west of Naples combined natural curiosities with classical sites familiar from the works of Cicero, Tacitus and Suetonius. The whole zone was redolent of Rome's foundation myths and the legend of Aeneas, celebrated by Virgil.

The discovery of Herculaneum in 1738 had an enormous impact throughout Europe. Horace Walpole wrote perceptively to his friend Richard West in June 1740, after visiting its theatre (below, p. 112).

Have you ever heard of the subterraneous town? A whole Roman town with all its edifices remaining under ground ... perhaps one of the noblest curiosities that ever has been discovered ... found out by chance about year and a half ago. They began digging, they found statues; they dug farther, they found more. The path is very narrow, just wide enough and high enough for one man to walk upright ... Except some columns, they found all the edifices standing upright in their proper situation ... a few paintings extremely fine ... We have not seen them as yet, as they are kept in the King's apartment [at Portici], whither all these curiosities are transplanted; and tis difficult to see them – but we shall ... I should be inclined to search for the other towns that were partners with this in the general ruin ... Tis certainly an advantage to the learned world, that this has been laid up so long. Many of the discoveries in Rome were made in a barbarous age, where they only ransacked the ruins in quest of treasure, and had no regard to the form and being of the building, or to any circumstances that might give light into its use and history.

Treasure-hunting nevertheless remained an important objective at this time and later.

Longer-term residents at Naples in the eighteenth century included Sir William Hamilton, Minister Plenipotentiary of King George III at the Royal Court in Naples from 1764 to 1800. His tenure coincided with a particularly active phase of volcanic activity (above, p. 20). Hamilton, whose passion for antiquities encompassed Greek and Roman vases, glassware and statuary, showed the sites to his house guests. When Admiral Nelson was convalescing in Naples under Emma Hamilton's care in 1793, his 13-year-old servant, William Hoste, later a dashing frigate captain, was given 'orders of admission' to visit Herculaneum and the Museum at Portici; but as the guides could not speak English or French, his 'curiosity was more excited than gratified'.

An ascent of Vesuvius was an obligatory excursion. Sir William Hamilton guided his visitors on to its slopes, some none too willingly, especially during or soon after an eruption. Artists and engravers depicted the volcano from every conceivable angle. The method of ascent varied. Visitors could be hauled upwards attached by a belt to a local guide, as was Goethe on 6 March 1787, or later carried by *portantini* in a sedan-chair, or rode on mules. The British were notorious for their rashness in climbing to the volcano's lip, for example James Boswell and John Wilkes in 1765, who lay flat on their stomachs peering over into the smoking crater.

On his return to Germany from a tour of Italy in 1766, Prince Leopold III Friedrich Franz of Anhalt-Dessau, who had been shown over Vesuvius by Sir William Hamilton, built an artificial volcano on a lake in his estate at Wörlitz near Dresden, which could be made to erupt; it has recently been brought back into working order.

The Napoleonic War curtailed non-essential travel, but it resumed in 1815. Sir William Gell, cicerone at Naples to the aristocracy until his death in 1836, published the influential two-volume *Pompeiana* (1817–19), the first general account in English, with a series of valuable illustrations for the armchair tourist, in conjunction with the architect J.P. Gandy. In January 1832 Gell showed the Palace of the Spirits at Posillipo (below, p. 81) to the ailing novelist Sir Walter Scott from a boat offshore. The anonymous author of *Notes on Naples* warned in 1838 against 'a bevy of guides, who look out in autumn and winter for travellers, as fowlers for game … at the gates of Pozzuoli.'

There are many travellers' accounts of Vesuvius. In 1819 the poet Shelley wrote that a

> thick heavy white smoke is perpetually rolled out, interrupted by enormous columns of an impenetrable black bituminous vapour, which is hurled up, fold after fold, into the sky with a deep hollow sound, and fiery stones are rained down from its darkness, and a black shower of ashes fell even where we sat. The lava, like the glacier, creeps on perpetually, with a crackling sound as of suppressed fire.

The essayist Anna Jameson, ascending in 1822, had to move quickly in quite unladylike fashion to sidestep 'an immense red-hot stone which came bounding down the mountain'. The sketchbook of the artist J.M.W. Turner was sprinkled with hot ash as he ascended in 1828. In the same year, Craufurd Tait Ramage and his party were actually standing on the crater's lip when part of its rim opposite them collapsed in upon itself. Charles Dickens climbed the mountain by moonlight in February 1845, the ice-covered slopes during his visit contrasting with the sheets of fire rising from the crater itself, reddening the night sky. In his guidebook of 1853 for the publisher John Murray, Octavian Blewitt recommended a particular guide for the ascent.

> His qualifications are so well known that there are numerous imposters ready to personify him, and the only way to avoid this deception is to go direct to his residence in the main street of Resina [modern Ercolano], or to write before-hand to secure him.

Travel was a leisurely activity, if uncomfortable and sometimes dangerous. Visitors were advised to spend between four and six weeks in Naples. They progressed between the sites in carriages, riding horses or mules, or by sea. The playwright and travel writer Mariana Starke, recording her experiences in 1797, advised day-trippers from Naples to allow four hours for reaching Sorrento by boat, four or five hours for resting the oarsmen, and four for returning.

Wealthy travellers arranged for the transport home of ancient artworks and statues which they purchased in Naples or at the sites, or commissioned sculptors to reproduce them; painters such as Jakob Hackert were on hand to depict the landscape, for the decoration of their town houses or country mansions. Cork models of the sites or individual buildings could be purchased; examples are preserved at Sir John Soane's house, now a museum, in Lincoln Inn's Fields, London. Sir John Clerk of Penicuik – in Italy during the final years of the seventeenth century – brought home 'a piece of an old Roman's skin, which I cut off a body in the catacombs of Naples.' Samples of lava from the slopes of Vesuvius found their way to many homes in Britain, and soon to museum collections. The youthful Frederick Howard, Fifth Earl of Carlisle, apologised to a friend in a letter from Naples in May 1768:

> I was extremely delighted by the Museum [at Portici] of the things taken out of Herculaneum, but could steal nothing for you, and it is very difficult to buy anything of the workmen, as there is a guard always over them when they

dig, to prevent them from concealing anything of value. At Rome I shall take pains to get you something.

Such depredations are not merely the stuff of past generations. Recent decades have seen the theft of gold jewellery from the site museum at Herculaneum and of statuettes from the garden of the House of the Vettii at Pompeii. Wall paintings still in situ have been spirited away, as was a heavy stone wine-press from a villa east of Vesuvius in 2007.

The discovery of Herculaneum and then Pompeii had a considerable impact on interior design and decorative arts, within the broader context of the neoclassical movement, especially following the publication at Naples under the royal imprint of the multi-volume *Antichità di Ercolano* (1757–71); an English translation of part of it soon followed. The interiors of Pompeian houses were reconstructed in European capitals. The painter Sir Lawrence Alma-Tadema cumulatively spent several weeks at Pompeii, first on his honeymoon in 1863. The site and its wall-paintings exerted a powerful influence on his genre paintings of the Roman world.

Travellers in the nineteenth century, increasingly also from the US, included the poet Henry Wadsworth Longfellow in 1828, and the novelist James Fenimore Cooper in 1829 (below, p. 154). Mark Twain, who came all the way from New York on a cruise ship in 1867, felt himself privileged to land on the mole at Pozzuoli at the precise spot where St Paul had disembarked in AD 61.

From the 1860s the mass travel pioneer Thomas Cook was conducting parties to Pompeii and independent travellers subsequently expressed their relief at being able to fall back upon Cook's representative at Naples in time of trouble or distress (*12*). The American novelist Francis Marion Crawford (1854–1909), long resident in a seafront villa at Sant'Agnello outside Sorrento, described in 1894:

> the Cook's tourist, the German water-color painter, or the English spinster, all of whom come yearly southward to the Sorrento coast, as regular in their migration as the swallow, and far more welcome to the bankrupt hotel-keeper and the starving boatman ... They come, they eat, they sleep, and their scarlet guide-books catch the sun and mark them for the native's prey.

It was all the fault of the publisher John Murray of Albemarle Street in London.

12 Ascending Vesuvius on the funicular railway, *c.*1880. (Giacomo Brogi; courtesy of L. Keppie)

Mr Murray says to the tourist, 'Go', and he goeth, or, 'Do this', and he doeth it, in the certain consciousness that he cannot do wrong ... I will venture to say that the average tourist in Italy sees very little that is distinctively Italian.

His words can at times still ring true, more than a century later.

Allied servicemen, stationed for a time round the Bay in 1944, included the comedian Spike Milligan, the authors Raleigh Trevelyan, Norman Lewis and Leonard Cottrell who was hospitalised at Torre del Greco, and the poet Gavin Ewart who rewarded his guide at Pompeii with a tin of corned beef. All have left us a written record of their experiences.

Since the Second World War, and especially from the 1960s onwards, large-scale tourism has brought an ever growing number of holidaymakers to the Bay. Most are now transported to their destinations in a few hours by air, and their sojourns are relatively brief when compared with their predecessors of a century and more ago. Visitor numbers at Pompeii now top two million a year, with an inevitable impact on the ancient remains and the modern infrastructure.

two

Visiting Roman Sites on the Bay

1. Ischia

The holiday island of Ischia (Pithecusae to the Greeks, then Roman Aenaria) is famed for its beaches and numerous cure-hotels, testimony to its hot springs (*13*). Ancient authors refer to earthquakes and volcanic eruptions, and an associated tsunami during the fourth century BC. The harbour itself, Ischia Porto, is in origin a small crater, opened to the sea only in 1854. Ischia is reached by frequent ferries from Pozzuoli and Naples, and currently once daily from Sorrento. Local buses circle the island in clockwise and anti-clockwise directions. Modern development has swept over the island, and what can sometimes appear on quite recent maps as open countryside has succumbed to ribbon development.

Ischia witnessed the earliest known settlement of Greek colonists on 'mainland' Italy (as opposed to Sicily), at Monte Vico above Lacco Ameno on the island's north coast, dating to the eighth century BC. By contrast Roman activity was centred further much further east, at Cartaromana Bay

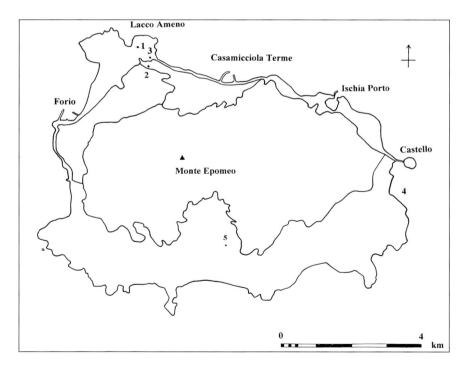

13 Ischia: 1. Monte Vico; 2. Museo Archeologico di Pithecusae; 3. Church of S. Restituta; 4. Cartaromana Bay; 5. Nitrodi Springs

south of the Castello Aragonese which, before it was linked to the mainland, occupied an island, in origin a volcanic plug (*13*).

The visitor in search of archaeology needs to head by bus north-westwards from Ischia Porto to Lacco Ameno. Displays at the Museo Archeologico di Pithecusae housed in the eighteenth-century Villa Arbusto, at 210 Corso Angelo Rizzoli, set the substantial Greek settlement in the context of trade patterns throughout the Mediterranean. (Hours: 9.30–13.00, 15.00–19.00, winter; 16.00–20.00, summer; closed Mondays.) Accessible also from Via Circumvallazione on the bus route. An important exhibit is the two-handled 'Nestor's Cup' of the eighth century BC with its early Greek inscription. Roman material on view includes lead sling bullets, lamps and glassware from tombs, and several large anchors. Inscribed lead and tin ingots from a foundry owned by the Atellii family from Puteoli were found by underwater exploration in Cartaromana Bay. A dozen marble reliefs (represented here by casts), dedicated to Apollo and the *Nymphae Nitrodes*, were found in 1757 at the Nitrodi Springs nearer the south coast of the island; the originals were carried off immediately to Naples. Dedicants include a freedwoman of the empress Poppaea Augusta, wife of Nero.

Excavations below the church of S. Restituta (in Piazza Restituta near the harbour) from 1951 onwards revealed not only a fourth-century Early Christian basilica, but underlying Greek and Roman structures which have been laid out for viewing in a surprisingly extensive series of spaces. Look for the museum of religious material to one side of the church's brightly painted façade, and then follow signs for the '*scavi*'. (Hours: 9.30–12.30, Monday–Saturday.) The area now below the church was given over in Greek times to industrial activities evidenced by a series of kilns for tile and pottery manufacture from the seventh century BC onwards, and then to a Roman building optimistically interpreted as a temple. By the second century AD much of the area was given over to burials which continued in the Early Christian period and after. Finds from the site, and elsewhere on the island, are on view.

2. Cuma

The earliest known Greek settlement on the Italian mainland itself was at Cumae, now Cuma, geographically just beyond the confines of this guidebook. However, its extensive territory in antiquity encompassed

Baiae, Lake Avernus, the Lucrine Lake and (before the mid first century AD) Misenum. For the visitor by public transport from Naples, a likely start point could be the train station at Pozzuoli (below, p. 69) in the higher part of that town. From there local orange buses run to Bacoli, and a small shuttle bus links Miseno with Cuma, interconnecting with the above. If travelling by car, use the Tangenziale motorway to the Cuma exit. Alternatively, for those staying on Ischia, the car ferry brings them to the seafront at Pozzuoli. The site (*14*) is approached by climbing Via Monte di Cuma, which branches off the Strada Provinciale Vecchia Licola. Cars can be parked at the site entrance.

The hilltop of Cumae (or its 'acropolis', meaning any 'high town' or citadel, not just in Athens) with its breathtaking views was dominated by a temple aligned east–west, which has traditionally been ascribed to Jupiter; it was transformed later into a Christian basilica with baptismal font. (Hours: 9.00 – 1 hour before sunset. Closed 1 January, 1 May and 25 December.) The ticket issued at Cuma, valid for two consecutive days, allows admission at no extra cost to the archaeological park at Baia, the amphitheatre at Pozzuoli and the Museo Archeologico dei Campi Flegrei (Museum of the Phlegraean Fields) at the Castello di Baia (below, p. 63). On a lower terrace a temple to Apollo

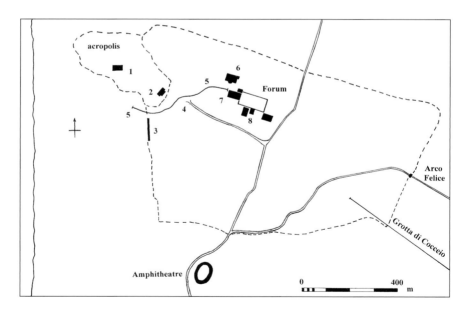

14 Cuma: 1. Temple of Jupiter; 2. Temple of Apollo; 3. Sibyl's Cave; 4. Entrance to site; 5. Grotta Romana; 6. Baths; 7. *Capitolium*; 8. Temples. (After Pagano 1986, with additions)

15 Cumae, columns in the porch of the Temple of Apollo. (James J. Walker)

was originally orientated north-east to south-west; but under Augustus a columned porch was added on its south-eastern side overlooking the town (15). This temple too was remodelled later as a Christian basilica, with burials inserted below its floor. The result is a confusing arrangement of columns and the juxtaposition of different building materials.

Cumae was one of the localities associated in antiquity with those ubiquitous prophetesses, the sibyls. At Cumae the sibyl inhabited a cave on the slope of the acropolis, and was inspired by the god Apollo or, as it may be, by gases rising from fissures in the rocks below. Antiquaries had originally equated her cave with the Grotta della Sibilla at Lago d'Averno (below, p. 69), and modern scholars with the dramatically engineered angular passageway on the lower terrace at Cuma itself near the Temple of Apollo. Cut into the rock along an escarpment, with regular openings for light on its seaward side, the passageway was later deepened to act as a cistern. However, doubts on its true purpose have recently been expressed; an initial military function has been suggested.

The extensive Graeco-Roman town on the plain to the east was enclosed by walls of which some traces can be made out. The *Via Domitiana* entered the town on its north flank, and left it to the east at the Arco Felice, a monumental brick-built archway, where the road slips through a gap in the foothills of Monte Grillo. Some of its paving is visible.

Public buildings were ranged round the Forum, where recent excavations have added to our knowledge. The high podium of a large temple dominates one end; originally marble clad, the building was modified in the first century AD to serve as a *Capitolium* when the town was, it seems, promoted to the status of colony. The extramural amphitheatre lies 700m south of the main site, to one side of the Strada Provinciale Arco Felice; the oval arena is now given over to horticulture. It may have been built before the end of the second century BC or at the beginning of the first. Unlike other sites on the Bay, the town of Cumae has remained in open countryside following abandonment in the thirteenth century. A sheltered harbour is postulated below the citadel. The cemeteries of Cumae have yielded many fine vases and sculptures, principally from the period of Greek settlement.

A tunnel through the tufaceous rock, the Crypta Romana, linked the harbour to the town, running below the acropolis. Currently closed for safety reasons, its entrance can be viewed from above. From the town another tunnel (the Grotta di Cocceio) led off eastwards under Monte Grillo in the direction of Lago d'Averno (see p. 69 for its terminus there); it was used to store munitions in the Second World War, to its permanent disfigurement.

We might have expected the coastline hereabouts, north-west of Capo di Miseno, to have been lined with Roman villas; some meagre traces survive above a substantial lake, Virgil's *Acherusia palus*, nowadays the Lago di Fusaro. A small island near the lake's eastern shore is occupied by the Casina Reale built by Carlo Vanvitelli for King Ferdinand of Naples as a fishing lodge in 1782; later it served as a marine biological station and is now sometimes used for exhibitions.

On the coast at Torregaveta, at the southern end of the Lago di Fusaro near the terminus of the Cumana and Circumflegrea railways, a rocky promontory now partly overlain by modern buildings and much altered by quarrying is the site of a villa which at one time was the place of retirement of Servilius Vatia, senator under Augustus. Seneca, writing some 50 years later, recounts how he often passed it, while journeying in a litter from Cumae to Baiae. Seneca never went inside the villa and was familiar only with its façade onto the road, but features then visible to the passerby included two grottoes and a fish-filled water channel. The few remaining walls, in *opus reticulatum* belonging to the Late Republic or Early Empire, give little hint of its one-time sophistication.

3. Miseno

The distinctive flat-topped Capo di Miseno is visible from afar round the Bay, even from Sorrento and Capri on clear days, most impressively towards sunset. The hill itself remains largely free of development except for a modern lighthouse, accessed through a tunnel (*16*). At sea level on the landward side a close-packed array of restaurants, bars and kiosks caters for the many Italian families holidaying on adjacent beaches. In legend the promontory took its name from the trumpeter Misenus, one of Aeneas' mythical shipmates, drowned there by the sea-god Triton; the hilltop bears

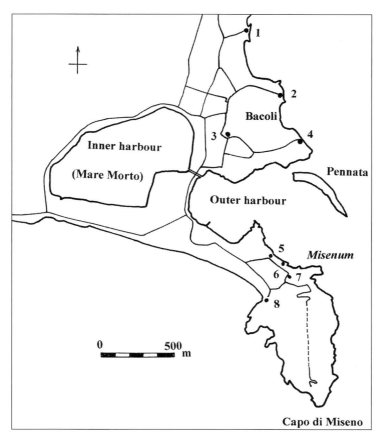

16 Bacoli and Miseno: 1. Tomb of Agrippina; 2. Cento Camerelle; 3. Piscina Mirabilis; 4. Lighthouse; 5. Theatre; 6. Shrine of the *Augustales*; 7. Baths; 8. Grotta della Dragonara. (After Amalfitano et al. 1990)

some resemblance to a circular burial mound of the type with which Virgil's readers would have been familiar. This was almost certainly another volcanic plug.

Though the summit seems ideal for a Roman villa, few traces have ever been found and flanks of the hill have long since been defaced by quarrying. This must be the likeliest location for a villa attested in the literary sources, built by Gaius Marius, then owned by Cornelia, daughter of Sulla, then by Lucullus, and later in imperial ownership. Emperor Tiberius, heading one last time for Capri, died there in March AD 37, allegedly smothered with a pillow by the praetorian prefect Sutorius Macro. Excavation has been in progress on the lower slopes of the promontory, where a series of rooms are identifiable, close to a Roman cistern known as the Grotta della Dragonara, fed by a freshwater spring. (At the far end of Via Dragonara, where the sandy beach gives way to the sloping side of Capo di Miseno.)

From the Augustan period onwards, the land around Capo di Miseno was given over to a naval base which took advantage of a double basin, one open to the sea and the other enclosed, but linked by a canal once crossed by a wooden bridge. The basins were in origin volcanic craters. The broad mouth of the outer basin was screened by concrete breakwaters. Little is known of any barracks; perhaps some crews slept aboard their ships. Misenum became an independent township under Claudius, hived off from Cumae. Archaeologically little now remains of what must have been a very crowded locality, south of the outer basin. Public buildings, including a theatre and baths, were shoe-horned into it.

One of the most exciting discoveries at Miseno in recent decades has been the Sacello degli Augustali (*Sacellum* of the *Augustales*), a sculpture-rich shrine facing the Forum. (From the Grotta della Dragonara on the Spiaggia di Miseno, turn right to cross the base of the promontory to Via Faro.) Established under Augustus, the *Sacellum* was remodelled in the Antonine period, but it was buried by a landslip around the end of the second century AD, preserving in situ statues of Vespasian, Titus, and Domitian, now on view in the museum at Castello di Baia (below). A number of statue bases dedicated to emperors, divinities and prominent *Augustales* were found in front of the temple. The brick-faced concrete structures of the *Sacellum* are visible from the street on Via Faro (*colour plate 3*). There are Roman remains too on the narrow islet of Pennata, originally the rim of a crater (the modern name reflecting its wing-shape), which was severed from the mainland following storms in 1966–67.

Northwards from the naval basins, the coastline, which went by the name of Bauli (now the seaside resort of Bacoli), was adorned in antiquity with a sequence of luxury villas. Underground cisterns on two levels served a villa sometimes identified as the one owned hereabouts by the orator Hortensius, Cicero's bitter rival in the law courts of Rome in the mid-first century BC. The modern name, Cento Camerelle ('Hundred Roomlets'), reflects the multiple

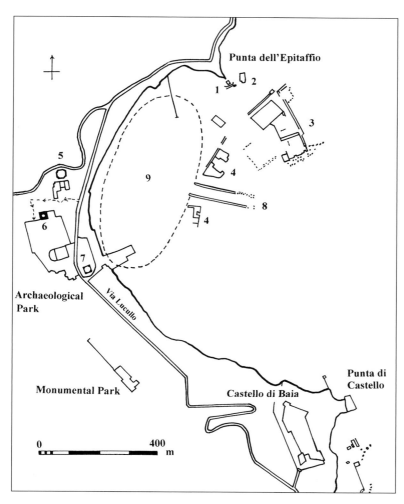

17 Baiae: 1. *Nymphaeum*; 2. Baths; 3. Villa of the Pisones; 4. Villa; 5. 'Temple of Diana'; 6. 'Temple of Mercury'; 7. 'Temple of Venus'; 8. Access channel to lake; 9. Baian lake (After Amalfitano et al. 1990, with additions)

compartments. (Near the east end of Via Centocamerelle; the address of the keyholder is posted at the gate.) Only meagre traces remain of the villa which once sat atop the cisterns. Brick-faced walling of a square tower on the coast is suggested as a lighthouse. Another villa, named in local tradition as the Sepolcro di Agrippina (Tomb of Agrippina), Nero's mother who was buried hereabouts along the coast after she was murdered in AD 59 (above, p. 30), boasted a small theatre, later converted to an ornamental water feature, a *nymphaeum*, so losing its original function. (Hours: 9.00 – 1 hour before sunset, or enquire about access at the adjacent Ristorante Garibaldi.)

Particularly rewarding for the modern visitor is a gigantic cistern, quarried from the natural rock, the so-called Piscina Mirabilis ('amazing pool'). This gigantic waterproofed cavern, in internal appearance like an underground basilica with rows of connecting archways supported on columns of volcanic tuff, held some 12600m³ of water, and was presumably the naval base's prime water supply fed by the Aqua Augusta. (On Via Piscina Mirabile, with the address of the keyholder posted at the gate; disabled access.) The Piscina Mirabilis featured strongly in Robert Harris' recent novel *Pompeii*. The visitor by public transport can now take a local orange bus from its nearby terminus to Bacoli, changing there for another to Pozzuoli, then the blue SEPSA bus, or the metro, for Naples.

4. Baia

A journey of a few kilometres northwards brings the visitor to Roman Baiae, once described by Horace as the 'loveliest bay in the world', but which changes to the shoreline and piecemeal development, together with modern commercial use, have reduced to a shadow of its former beauty (*17*). The visitor coming from Miseno will first see the Castello di Baia, dramatically positioned on a headland. Built by Alfonso d'Aragona in the later fifteenth century, it was extended by Don Pedro de Toledo, the Spanish viceroy at Naples, in the sixteenth. After abandonment as a military fortification, the castle was given over to other uses, including an orphanage; later it served as accommodation for people left homeless after the earthquake of 1980.

The sprawling Castello now houses the Museo Archeologico dei Campi Flegrei. (Hours: 9.00 – 1 hour before sunset. Closed Mondays and 1 January, 1 May and 25 December.) One hall houses, rather uncomfortably, the reconstructed façade of the Sacello degli Augustali at Miseno, in which stand heroic nude statues of Vespasian and his elder son Titus, both immediately recognisable, together with a quite remarkable bronze equestrian statue of the younger son, Domitian, reconstructed from surviving fragments. The head was reworked on Domitian's death (and 'damnation') in AD 96 to represent his much older successor Nerva. The mounted figure originally held a javelin and so was being shown in victorious military pose, as often on coins of Domitian's reign. On the pediment of the reconstructed facade are portrait busts in relief of the freedman L. Laecanius Primitivus and his wife Cassia Victoria who financed rebuilding in AD 161–65, as the inscription on the architrave proudly proclaims.

On a higher floor, reached by following the wooden walkway, are reconstructed elements of a *nymphaeum* of likely Claudian date, from Punta dell'Epitaffio to the north of Baia (below, p. 67). The principal statue group depicted Odysseus in the cave of the cyclops Polyphemus, while niches in the side-walls were occupied by statues of Dionysus, god of wine and fertility, and of the Julio-Claudian imperial family. Diners reclined on marble couches of which parts of two survive, facing a central pool in what was in effect an artificial grotto, with fountains and cascades lit by torches, selecting, it has been suggested, from delicacies which floated towards them on miniature galleys. One end of the hall was partly open on to the Bay. Small finds are displayed in adjacent cases, together with a model of the building as found. There is also a large wall-mounted relief map of the area.

Inscribed statue bases from the Sacello degli Augustali displayed on the castle terraces include dedications to emperors from Nerva to Marcus Aurelius. Marine deities and sailing vessels, sculpted on their side-faces, emphasise the importance to the *Augustales* of seaborne trade which the fleet protected. There is a large wall-mounted plaque honouring the American scholar John H. D'Arms who gave so much of his energy to elucidating Roman society on the Bay (above p. 13). The dormitory wing of the castle, on two floors, contains archaeological finds from Roman Puteoli, including from the excavations in its Rione Terra (below, p. 71). Development as a visitor attraction continues. From the castle terraces there are fine views across the Bay of Baia to Pozzuoli on its promontory some 4km distant. The visitor has the chance here to judge the length of the bridge of boats built from nearby Bauli (modern Bacoli) to Puteoli in AD 39 on Caligula's instructions (above, p. 39).

The headland occupied by the Castello di Baia is the likely location of a villa once owned by Julius Caesar, which we know from Tacitus offered views not only over the Bay but southwards towards Bacoli and Miseno. Excavation in the substructures of the Castello has revealed Roman flooring of the Late Republic onwards. Other structures have been identified against the sea-facing cliffs below the Castello and in front of it at sea level. Caesar's villa presumably became imperial property and can be identified as one of the emperors' principal residences at Baiae.

Baiae was the Bay's most famous resort, and is remarked upon by many ancient authors down to the Late Empire. People visited Baiae to 'take the waters', like Augustus' daughter Julia, and his ill-fated nephew Marcellus who died at Baiae in 23 BC. The very name was long redolent of debauchery. Cicero in 56 BC could link 'orgies, flirtations, Baiae, beach parties, riotous dinners, revels, musical entertainments, concerts and boating parties' in his stinging courtroom castigation of the noblewoman Clodia's dissolute lifestyle. A century later Seneca – who was glad to leave Baiae after only a day – railed against drunks swaying along the foreshore, noisy shipboard parties and raucous music echoing round the bay. The poet Martial knew of Laevina, a woman of high morals, who arrived at Baiae a Penelope, the virtuous wife of Odysseus, and left a Helen of Troy, seduced by the waters, abandoning her husband for a much younger man.

The present-day shoreline, with its jetties, barges and yacht berthings, does not represent the ancient coast, which underwater investigations have shown extended to a distance of 370m out from the modern shore. Villas fringed an oval lake (presumably another crater like Avernus and Lucrine to the north-east), which was connected to the sea by a broad channel north of the present-day quays (*17*). It is easy to forget that nowadays we are passing through the middle of the Roman resort rather than skirting its eastern edge.

The modern visitor comes to Baia principally to see the extensive remains housed in the Archaeological Park. (Via Sella di Baia, 22; on the right of the road, i.e. uphill, when coming from Pozzuoli, almost opposite the currently defunct train station on the Cumana line. Hours: 9.00 – 1 hour before sunset. Closed 1 January, 1 May, 25 December.) The site is distinctive for its series of large, seemingly isolated rotundas, important in the study of Roman architectural forms (*18*). Interpreted by early visitors as temples, hence the modern names applied to them, we now see them as parts of baths-complexes spread out across the hillside, fed by hot thermal springs. The intact 'Temple of Mercury' is the earliest, dating from the reign of Augustus. Site plans often omit the roofless, Hadrianic 'Temple of Venus', on the other side of the modern road and outside the boundaries of the

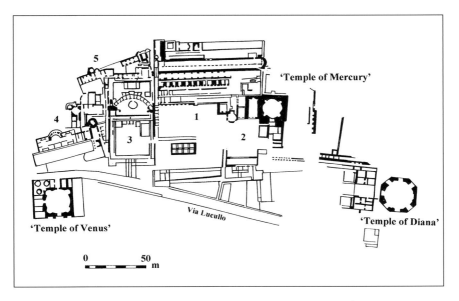

18 Baiae, the Archaeological Park: 1.Villa of the Promenade; 2. Sector of Mercury; 3. Sector of Sosandra; 4. Sector of Venus; 5. Minor Baths. (After McKay 1967)

Archaeological Park (*colour plate 4*).The 'Temple of Diana', likewise divorced from the main site, is latest in date, built in the mid–third century AD.

The site-plan depicts a bewildering array of gardens, fountains, arcades and porticoes, residential accommodation and service wings across the hillside, all the subject of frequent renovation, reconstruction and remodelling in ancient times. Some elements could have belonged originally to private properties. Information panels located at the entrance and across the site help with orientation. The site is divided into sectors, to make comprehension easier.

Likely to be noticed first is the octagonal 'Temple of Diana', of which half the dome survives, as it is readily visible from the access road. Inside the Archaeological Park the visitor arrives first at the Villa dell'Ambulatio (Villa of the Promenade) on expansive terraces, then to the 'Sector of Mercury', named for its principal feature, the huge 'Temple of Mercury', which the sinking of the ground here has submerged to the base of the intact dome.

To the south lies the 'Sector of Sosandra' (named for a statue of Aphrodite Sosandra found there, a Roman copy of an original on the Acropolis in Athens), a clearly defined east–west strip sloping down towards the sea,

19 Baiae, semicircular arcade and circular bath in the Sector of Sosandra. (L. Keppie)

which includes residential and dining facilities; prominent is a semicircular arcade (*19*), with a circular pool in front, above a large garden, the latter recalling the porticoed courtyard beside the theatre at Pompeii (below, p. 134). Finally at the far southern end is the 'Sector of Venus', with bath suites on different levels, including the Minor Baths, a recognisable sequence of cold and heated rooms, the latter fed directly by waters from a spring in the hills behind. Lower down, at the south-east end, is a large, brick-faced apsed building of Hadrianic date, interpreted as a *nymphaeum*, close to the roofless 'Temple of Venus' on the far side of the modern road (*colour plate 4*).

The bath-complexes at Baiae have sometimes been identified as an enormous imperial villa, but the emperors' properties are better restricted to, or must certainly have included, the elevated and more exclusive setting of one or both of the twin promontories of Punta di Castello and Punta dell'Epitaffio (below p. 67) flanking the bay. Ample space remains on the hillsides for the many private villas which our sources also record.

A connecting path gives access to the separate Monumental Park where a lengthy portico stretched southwards along the crest of the ridge. Associated buildings can be dated to the early second century BC; additions were made in the Late Republic, and further enlargements later. Access can also be gained through a gate on Via Bellavista (with parking). Further south, other remains were recorded in advance of quarrying on the ridge leading to the Castello.

The Punta dell'Epitaffio at the northern end of the bay is marked by structural remains atop and along its cliffs, but much more lies out of sight beneath the waves. Underwater exploration in 1959–60, again in the 1980s and from 1998 onwards, revealed an array of structures hitherto unsuspected. Immediately out to sea beyond the Punta was a *nymphaeum*, in fact the dining room of a sumptuous villa, of likely Claudian date, from which the surviving statues, some of which were found still upright or had merely fallen from their plinths, can be seen in the museum at the Castello di Baia (above, p. 62). Close by was a suite of baths built during the Flavian period and, further out from the modern headland, a rectangular porticoed courtyard. From the discovery there of lead piping stamped with the name *L. Pisonis*, this property been identified as the villa owned hereabouts by the Calpurnii Pisones, an aristocratic family brought down when its chief representative ill-advisedly headed a botched conspiracy against Nero in AD 65; it was here that the conspirators proposed the Emperor be assassinated. No part of the residential area of the villa has been located, and it is to be hoped that future work will bring further discoveries. The later history of Baiae was relatively undistinguished, and it slipped from the historical record to become, as the centuries passed, the stuff of myth and legend.

It is now possible for visitors to inspect some of the underwater archaeological remains and the rich aquatic life below the waves, either in subaqua gear or in a glass-bottomed boat. A 45-minute excursion aboard the boat *Cymba* – named after Charon's craft in which he ferried souls to the underworld – allows the viewing of the Villa of the Pisones seated in a rather cramped, glass-panelled compartment below the waterline. (Turn off the main coastal road, Via Lucullo, into Via Molo di Baia at the 'Temple of Venus', to reach the harbour. Advance booking on www.baiasommersa.it.) The boat trip also allows inspection of the present-day shoreline, where structural remains survive against the cliffs. Excursions in subaqua gear have the promise of an especially rewarding visit; information panels on the seabed explain the remains for the passing diver.

The northern flank of the present-day promontory, at Tritole beyond the Punta dell' Epitaffio, was similarly adorned with villas and with thermal establishments including the so-called Stufe di Nerone ('Nero's Ovens'), which are dramatically terraced against the hillside, and which tapped into naturally occurring hot springs.

5. Lago di Lucrino and Lago d'Averno

Continuing along the shore, the visitor soon reaches a strip of land separating what little now remains of the Lago di Lucrino (Lucrine Lake) from the modern shore. In ancient times the Lucrine was separated from the sea by a narrow causeway strengthened and raised in successive generations, as the sea began to wash over it. The buildings fringing its eastern shore – which we know included a villa belonging to Cicero, his beloved *Cumanum*, and another in the possession of the senatorial family of Nero's empress Poppaea – fell victim in 1538 to the emergent Monte Nuovo (above, p. 19).

The Lucrine was originally far more extensive, but shallow, and famed for its oyster beds first exploited in the first century BC by an entrepreneur Sergius Orata, also believed to have invented the hypocaust, the underfloor heating for bath-houses, a development easily linked to the presence of hot springs hereabouts. In the thirties of the first century BC, Vipsanius Agrippa, acting for Octavian, the soon-to-be emperor Augustus, converted the Lucrine Lake and Lake Avernus behind it into naval harbours named *Portus Iulius* in Octavian's honour. He cut a canal to link the Avernus to the Lucrine, then the latter to the sea by a long channel near its eastern end, felling the enclosing woodland, with little respect for Avernus' mythical associations with Aeneas and the underworld. The naval base proved short-lived, as land movements soon rendered the channels unusable for large vessels; the fleet was transferred to Capo di Miseno (above, p. 59) where it was to remain for several centuries.

Agrippa's works along the seafront would have remained unsuspected but for the fact that the sinking of the land relative to the sea in post-Roman times submerged them, to be revealed again by aerial photography and underwater prospection. Stone-built warehouses and docks vividly demonstrate the extent of the construction work undertaken eastwards towards Puteoli; but there is nothing now for the terrestrial visitor to see. However, the sunken remains hereabouts were celebrated by the poet Shelley, who in the winter of 1819, in his 'Ode to the West Wind', 'saw in sleep old palaces and towers / Quivering beneath the wave's intenser day / All overgrown with azure moss and flowers'.

Nowadays the Lucrine is quickly passed, its margins given over to restaurants and bars, but a road leads the modern visitor away at right angles from the coast to the nearby Lago d'Averno (Lake Avernus), on whose shores are a number of ruins, some associated with Agrippa and his works, and others now identified as bathing establishments. Lake Avernus was famed in antiquity as an entrance to the underworld, and long maintained an atmosphere of dark foreboding. Here Aeneas, the Trojan refugee newly landed in Italy, descended in Virgil's *Aeneid* to the banks of the River Styx, in the company of the Cumaean Sibyl (above, p. 57), where he met his father, various Trojan heroes, and his descendants down to Virgil's own time. The depths of the lake were investigated in 1989 with echo-sounding equipment and the coring of sediments.

Turning right (eastwards) on arrival at the Lago d'Averno, the visitor will encounter the 'Temple of Apollo', a hexagonal bath similar to those at Baiae, and frequently depicted by artists. In the other direction (westwards) along the lake's southern shore are structures known as the Navale di Agrippa (Agrippa's shipyard), and close by are some remnants thought to be a bathing suite, in use again in the Middle Ages. Here too was a tunnel (the Grotta della Sibilla) of which a length of 200m survives, heading for the Lucrine but truncated since the sixteenth century. (Enquire locally about access.) From the far northern side of the lake a second tunnel (the Grotta di Cocceio) headed westwards under Monte Grillo towards Cumae (above, p. 58). Both tunnels are presumed to be associated with Agrippa's works.

6. Pozzuoli

By the Early Empire Puteoli was the largest Roman town on the Bay, but only scattered massive monuments now attest to its significance (*20*). The place immediately demonstrates the very different fate to Pompeii and Herculaneum of a Roman town which continued to be occupied down to Late Antiquity, through the Middle Ages to the present day. Easy access in about 25 minutes on Line 2 of the metro from Naples Piazza Garibaldi train station, lower level, to the terminus at Pozzuoli; some trains continue to Formia. From the station at Pozzuoli, walk downhill on Via C. Rosini; the large amphitheatre soon comes into view. Alternatively use the Ferrovia Cumana railway from Napoli Montesanto station to its Pozzuoli halt in the lower part of town, convenient for Rione Terra (see below), the *Serapeum* and ferries for Ischia. Pozzuoli can also be reached by a bus direct from Piazza Garibaldi in Naples. By car, use the Tangenziale motorway round the north side of Naples, and the exit Pozzuoli-Via Campana.

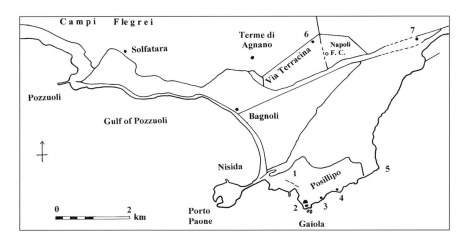

20 Gulf of Pozzuoli: 1. Grotta di Seiano; 2. Villa of Vedius Pollio; 3. Palace of the Spirits; 4. Church of S. Maria del Faro; 5. Capo di Posillipo; 6. Baths in Via Terracina; 7. 'Tomb of Virgil'

The nucleus of Roman Puteoli, indeed of the Greek settlement of Dicaiarchia which preceded it, was on a promontory jutting out into the Bay, now known as Rione Terra (*21*). Here stood a temple facing southwards out to sea, originally serving as the *Capitolium* of the Roman colony established in 194 BC, but later rededicated to the god Apollo. The belief that it was erected to Emperor Augustus is supposition, from an imaginative reconstruction of a lost inscription once visible on the facade. A second inscription names its freedman architect as L. Cocceius Auctus, likely to be identical to the inveterate tunneller.

In Late Antiquity the temple was converted to a church and became from the eleventh century the Cathedral of S. Proculo, the town's patron. In 1643 the church was reconstructed in Baroque style by its Spanish bishop, with side-chapels cut through the temple walls and the peripetal columns. In 1964 the Cathedral was badly damaged by fire, and again in 1970 by an earthquake. Subsequently it was decided to take down what remained to reveal the temple, but after the serious earthquakes in 1980 and 1983 the whole promontory was closed off and did not become accessible again on a regular basis until a few years ago. The inhabitants of the historic centre of the old town were moved to temporary accommodation.

The subsequent programme of stabilisation and restoration on the promontory has seen the development of a dramatic underground

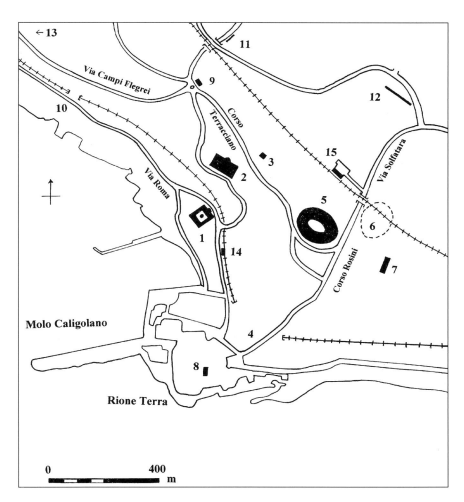

21 Pozzuoli, the principal monuments: 1. *Serapeum*; 2. *Thermae* of Neptune; 3. *Nymphaeum* of Diana; 4. Forum; 5. Amphitheatre; 6. Late Republican amphitheatre; 7. Piscina Cardito; 8. *Capitolium*; 9. Santa Marta; 10. Villa of Cicero; 11. Tombs along Via Celle; 12. Tombs along former Via Vecchia Vigna; 13. Stadium; 14. Train station (Cumana line); 15. Metro station. (After Amalfitano et al. 1990)

archaeological site, encompassing a network of walls, streets, shops, storage areas, slave accommodation and a shrine with wall-paintings of the Olympian Gods, all preserved below later buildings and connected by original stairs and modern walkways (*22*). Statues and their bases have also been recovered. The earliest structures are datable to the time of the colony's foundation in 194 BC, with later buildings in *opus reticulatum* and *opus latericium* (brick-faced concrete). The modern street-plan still reflects the layout of the Roman grid lying three metres below it. The Roman levels together with the temple – which has acquired a modern roof – are open at weekends for regular guided tours. (Access from Largo Sedile del Porto, signposted.) An on-site museum is planned.

Extending westwards out to sea below the promontory was a substantial mole, eventually 372m long and 15m wide, topped by archways and sculptural groups, whose gradually disintegrating remains are reported by antiquaries and repeatedly depicted by artists. Its arched piers remained visible into the twentieth century but are now enclosed within a modern breakwater. The Roman mole was a conspicuous feature of Puteoli, and the disembarkation point for many visitors from overseas. In AD 39 it served as

22 Pozzuoli, Roman buildings below ground in the Rione Terra

the eastern end of Caligula's famous bridge of boats formed across the Bay from Bauli (above, p. 30), hence the modern name of Molo Caligolano.

The importance of Puteoli in Roman times as a bustling mercantile centre may be hard to appreciate nowadays. However, a rich epigraphic record allows us to reconstruct its society and topography in some detail. The façades of many of its largest buildings (including a theatre, which has never been located on the ground) are usefully shown on engraved glass flasks, preserved in museums or private collections. Seemingly of fourth-century AD date, the flasks are interpreted as locally made souvenirs. Wax writing tablets found in a building at Moregine on the outskirts of Pompeii (below, p. 145) document the intense commercial activity.

The town – entitled *Colonia Iulia Augusta Puteoli*, later *Neronensis*, and subsequently *Flavia* (honouring the emperors Augustus, then Nero, then Vespasian) – was the principal entrepôt of corn intended for Rome and of much else besides, before the development of a port at Ostia near the mouth of the Tiber from Claudian times onwards. On what was to be his final trip to Capri in AD 14, Augustus' ship was passed in the Gulf of Puteoli by an Alexandrian vessel, whose crew and passengers saluted him as the revered originator of their prosperity. Seneca writes of the jubilation on the promenade when the annual grain fleet from Alexandria came into sight.

It is a brief northwards walk from Rione Terra along the seafront to the *Serapeum*, visible from the surrounding Piazza Serapide. In reality this was a market hall, named the Temple of Serapis for the discovery there in 1750 of a statue of the Egyptian god, now at Naples. Only in 1907 was the building correctly interpreted as a market. Built in brick-faced concrete (*opus latericium*), it belongs at the earliest under the Flavian emperors of the later first century AD.

This was, in essence, a square precinct facing the harbour, with porticoes on two storeys, their columns made of Egyptian granite from Syene, and, to the rear, of green cipollino marble from the Greek island of Euboea (*23*). Fish and meat shops faced inwards towards a circular fountain ringed by 16 columns in reddish Numidian marble with elaborate Corinthian capitals, their sculptured bases showing marine scenes. It is difficult now to envisage the original appearance of the building, with the loss of its marble cladding and most of the columns. An apse at the back probably contained the statue of Serapis; multi-seat toilets occupied the rear corner-angles.

Excavated between 1750–56 and 1806–18 by royal command as a source of column shafts and statuary for the new Palace at Caserta, the *Serapeum* was

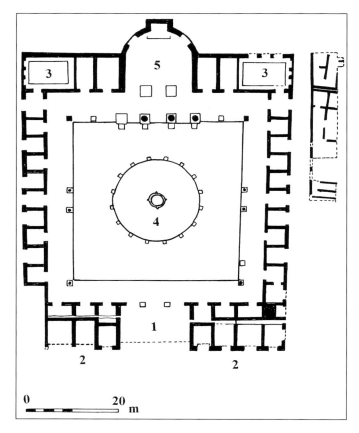

23 Pozzuoli, the *Serapeum*:
1. Vestibule;
2. Shops;
3. Latrines;
4. Fountain;
5. Apse. (After Amalfitano et al. 1990)

a landmark on the tourist itinerary even before Pompeii and Herculaneum were rediscovered. The site bears eloquent testimony to the rise and fall of the land hereabouts: the few remaining columns show the boreholes of sea molluscs in a band which extends up to 2.7m above the original market floor (24). The structure accordingly had a seminal importance for geologists, and was used as frontispiece of the first volume of Sir Charles Lyell's famous *Principles of Geology* (1830–33); he had seen the *Serapeum* on his travels in the volcano-rich zone. The visitor can turn now to admire the modern promenade, but the present writer remembers the seabed within the former harbourworks in use as a car park and open-air market, after the land had risen as much as 3m during the 1980s.

Behind the seafront the ground rises rapidly – the result of volcanic activity which created 'raised marine terraces'. Further uphill, the modern

24 Pozzuoli, the partially inundated *Serapeum*, 1979. (L. Keppie)

visitor arrives at the 'Temple of Neptune', now cheek by jowl with a modern prison. (Accessed from Corso Terracciano, 36.) In reality part of a large baths complex, datable by brickstamps to the reign of Hadrian (AD 117–38), its massive structures are on a par with the monumental *thermae* of Rome itself. On the far side of the street, the '*Nymphaeum* of Diana' preserves what could be further elements of the same baths; these and other remains nearby are now locked in by the security fences of adjacent condominiums.

A little to the east, still on Corso Terracciano, was a gigantic amphitheatre (*25*), the third largest known in the Roman world after the Colosseum in Rome and the amphitheatre at Capua, and the most important relic of the modern town's Roman past. (Hours: 9.00 – 1 hour before sunset. Closed Tuesdays, and 1 January, 1 May, 25 December.) The amphitheatre, which could have held up to 50,000 spectators, is dated to the Flavian period by inscriptions found above its entrances; but it may in fact have been inaugurated under Nero, who in AD 66 celebrated gladiatorial games at Puteoli in honour of King Tiridates of Armenia. The structure was topped by a ring of columns with statues set between them.

After viewing the arena and the partly restored seating, and noting the elongated pit in the arena-floor and the numerous small trapdoors which allowed animals to be raised into the arena from below, the visitor should make for the access ramp leading downwards to two floors of subterranean compartments (*colour plate 5*). The underground complex is amazingly intact, and one would think needs little more than fitting out with timber framing and plasterwork to bring it back into use. Architectural fragments, massive column capitals and fluted column shafts, some found at the site during nineteenth-century excavations, lie in the passageways. In addition many

25 Pozzuoli, looking towards the arena of the large amphitheatre

inscriptions, sculptures, sarcophagi and altars are arrayed near the main entrance to the site, for want of a museum which the town surely needs. On the far side of the modern street, opposite an entrance to the arena on the amphitheatre's south side, is a monumental fountain; water once poured from a lion-head mouth.

The town's Forum appears to have lain east of the promontory; some of its paving has been located by excavation and chance discoveries. Merchant families financed its laying out under Augustus, on a lavish scale appropriate to the town's increasing significance. To the north-east was another amphitheatre (not to be confused with the larger structure just described), orientated north-south and earlier than it in date, belonging perhaps to the mid-first century BC, but with later embellishments. Arches of its facade are most easily viewed from the train, on the right as it approaches Pozzuoli metro station from the east; they were cut through while that line was under construction in 1915.

The visitor with more time, preferably a second day to spend in the town, can seek out other surviving Roman remains amid modern buildings or incorporated into them, for example the Piscina Cardito, a rectangular cistern of second-century AD date which lies north-east of the Forum (entrance in Via Vecchia S. Gennaro, beyond modern flats; not currently open to visitors). Structures surviving within the recently redeveloped S. Marta complex at the far end of Corso Terracciano include a barrel-vaulted cistern with *opus reticulatum* facings.

Further west in the direction of the Lucrine Lake, elements of a bath building – traditionally identified as part of a villa belonging to Cicero who is known to have had a property hereabouts – protrude from shrubbery along Via Campi Flegrei, approximately 200m west of the roundabout at Piazza Capomazza. A few hundred metres further on was a brick-built stadium for athletics. One of the largest known at 260m in length, it is believed to have been constructed under Antoninus Pius to celebrate games in memory of his predecessor Hadrian who died at nearby Baiae in AD 138.

We lack firm knowledge of any walls that might have enclosed the straggling Roman town, apart from those which originally defended the promontory itself. The town's cemeteries necessarily lay mainly to the north, some along the road towards Capua, which ran between the craters of Campiglione to the west and Cigliano to the east. A line of 14 contiguous tomb enclosures, dating from the Augustan period onwards, stretches impressively along the modern Via Celle, just beyond the road and rail bridge. Once neatly laid out for public viewing, they are now disappointingly overgrown. (For photographs of the tombs in pristine condition, see www.comune.pozzuoli. na.it.) A few more lie in private residential property on the other side of the street. Others can be found northwards on the same route at Fondo di Fraia, S.Vito, and further on at the village of Quarto, named for its site at the fourth milestone from the town. In 1992–97 a line of tombs, surviving up to 3m high in a narrow, hitherto undeveloped corridor of land 400m north of the train station, was spectacularly revealed along an east-west paved road, the 'Via Antiniana' (a name deriving from local tradition only), when the town's bypass was being laid out. Many of the tombs here, currently shielded by protective roofing, bear inscriptions identifying the deceased. Development as an archaeological park is a possibility.

The zone north and east of modern Pozzuoli is a patchwork of overlapping craters, with modern Neapolitan suburbs spreading undaunted into the interiors of some and onto the slopes of others. La Solfatara, a crater formed no more than 3000 or 4000 years ago, has in recent times been active, but is by no means the largest. The sometimes smelly and sticky landscape of the Solfatara was celebrated in antiquity as the god Vulcan's workshop, and was long the site of a small geological observatory. (Via Solfatara, 161; by bus, use the direct service from Naples, heading for Pozzuoli, or a local shuttle; by car, leave the Tangenziale motorway at the Agnano exit. Hours: 8.30 – 1 hour before sunset, every day.)

The crater of Astroni immediately to the north attracts both geologists and botanists, the latter for the variety of the plant-life nourished by volcanically enriched soils. The even larger crater at Agnano, drained in 1870 and in part now occupied by a horse-racing course, was the scene of a celebrated spectacle for the tourist in earlier centuries, who came here to view the Grotta del Cane (Cave of the Dog). Richard Lassels who had seen the place in 1650 recorded that

A man takes a dog alive, and holding downe his head with a woodden forke to the ground, the dog begins first to cry, and then to turn up the white of the eyes, as if he would dye. Then letting him hold up his head againe, he recovers. And haveing thus twice, or thrice, shown us the experience of this infectious place, he putts downe the dogs head againe, and holds it down solong, till the dog seems to be dead indeed. Then taking him by the stiff leg, and running with him to the Lake Agnano, some forty paces off, he throws him into the shallow water of this Lake, and presently he begins to recover, and to wade out.

Lassels also notes that, unsurprisingly, dogs there 'runn whineing away when they see a troup of strangers arrive'; his book includes a woodcut illustrating the phenomenon. Tourists were charged an extra fee to see the 'dog experiment'. The Grotta, near the modern Nuove Terme d'Agnano, had a permanent fill of carbon dioxide, and long continued to attract the morbidly fascinated. The diarist John Evelyn in 1645 states that Turkish slaves had at one time been subjected to the same experiment. The architect Robert Adam and later the author Mark Twain have also left us graphic accounts; however, the spectacle was increasingly frowned upon in the guidebooks. On the crater's south-western slope an extensive Roman bathing establishment of Hadrianic date was revealed in 1898; from it came several fine statues placed on view at the Nuove Terme d'Agnano. Substantial structures survive against the hillside.

7. Posillipo

Beyond Pozzuoli the Bay bends again to the south, to the island of Nisida and the lofty headland of Posillipo, an area which until recent decades was largely free of urban sprawl and marked only by aristocratic mansions on the coastal cliffs. Now the land is almost completely built over from Bagnoli to Mergellina.

Modern road and rail links pass across the lower ground to the north, where redundant steelworks and other industrial premises await redevelopment. Local buses from the centre of Naples pass the island of Nisida on their way to Bagnoli, and others ascend to a terminus in Piazza Capo di Posillipo. Alternatively, the metro (Line 2) has a station at Cavalleggeri d'Aosta, from which a local bus brings the visitor along Via P. Leonardi Cattolica to Nisida.

The gourmet Lucullus, remembered nowadays less for his military achievements in the Middle East and Asia Minor in 74–66 BC than for the excesses of his subsequent retirement, owned a villa on Nisida. A few columns of unknown provenance are incorporated into the dungeons of medieval and later structures on the island, which has served as a prison and later as a youth offenders centre, linked to the mainland by a relatively modern causeway. The island had its own mini-crater, the Porto Paone. Several ancient authors report that Lucullus, at one of his properties near

Naples, cut through a mountain at great expense, to bring seawater directly to his beloved fish stocks, earning himself the nickname 'Xerxes in a toga', after the Persian king who had dug through the peninsula of Athos in Northern Greece in 483 BC to allow his fleet safe passage. Exactly how this could have been achieved, or indeed was actually topographically necessary at any of the villa-sites on the Bay associated with his name, eludes us. One attractive suggestion is that in fact Lucullus cut through the lip of the crater of Porto Paone on Nisida, to admit seawater to its interior.

The headland opposite Nisida is known as Posillipo, a name which derives from *Pausilypon* ('Free of Care' or 'Sans Souci'), accorded in the Augustan period to a villa there by its then owner, the notoriously cruel P. Vedius Pollio. The name has endured to this day. Vedius, who had grown rich from exploiting tax revenues in Asia Minor, bequeathed the villa at Posillipo, with his other properties, to Augustus in 15 BC and it remained in imperial ownership thereafter. In its fully developed form, the villa was draped across the hilltop and the cliffs below, incorporating the islets of Gaiola. The remains, valuably planned in 1897–1907 by Oxford zoologist R.T. Gunther, included a 2000-seater theatre, a small covered theatre (an *odeum*), baths and water cisterns. The Centro Studi Interdisciplinari Gaiola organises regular visits to the terrestrial archaeological remains, and, using scuba equipment, to marine life and submerged sites beyond the headland; the visitor must book in advance via its website (www.gaiola.org).

The principal access to the villa from the landward side in Roman times, and for the modern visitor, is via a 770m-long tunnel, the so-called Grotta di Seiano (on Discesa Coroglio, close to the causeway to Nisida), with side-shafts providing air and light (*colour plate 6*). The tunnel required strengthening in Bourbon times. Just beyond the tunnel's eastern end is a small cemetery, in use from the Augustan period onwards, perhaps the burial place of slaves and freedmen who staffed the villa.

The formerly much overgrown remains are currently being consolidated and attractively restored by the Superintendency of Antiquities. The theatre with 18 tiers of seating is immediately visible; a sunken water feature in front may once have been crowned by a restored statue of a sea nymph, now at Naples. The covered *odeum* lay opposite on the same alignment as the theatre, and was fronted by a portico. Further east, a set of baths at sea level faced a small harbour, protected by a mole. Offshore were extensive fish tanks. This was a miniature city, bringing to mind the villa and gardens of the aesthete Gabriele d'Annunzio at Gardone Riviera on Lake Garda.

Some remnants of this and other villas, in an arc between Nisida and the picturesque fishing harbour of Marechiaro – where Roman material is incorporated into the church of S. Maria del Faro – are best viewed from the sea. Notable is the three-storey Palazzo dei Spiriti (Palace of the Spirits, named for a ghost which used to emerge out of one of the floors), from which boys nowadays leap fearlessly into the sparkling waters beneath (*colour plate 7*). Further east, off the actual Capo di Posillipo, are remains of a Roman villa which was built out over the sea below the Villa Rosebery, the latter owned at one time by Lord Rosebery, British Prime Minister during the period 1894–9; it is now the summer residence of the President of Italy.

The cliffs at Posillipo and the structures set against them have been the subject of innumerable etchings and paintings by generations of artists – among them Achille Gigante in the mid-nineteenth century – and remained one of the most sought after locations for a coastal villa almost to the present day. The two-year-old W.S. Gilbert, travelling with his parents, was abducted hereabouts in 1838 by banditti, according to family tradition, and subsequently ransomed for the sum of £25.

The Roman road linking Puteoli to Neapolis followed an inland route, along the southern flank of the crater of Agnano, then split; one branch struck out north-eastwards skirting the Vomero Hill and the Castel S. Elmo, while the other veered seawards. Beside the higher level road to Naples, on modern Via Terracina, a thermal complex of the second century AD found in 1939 fronts on to the Roman road, with walling surviving to a height of 1m or more. Sea creatures decorate the mosaic floors of the vestibule, the *apodyterium*, and a semicircular multi-seater latrine. The building retains some wall-mounted tubular tiles and hypocaust pillars of the type familiar to students of Roman Britain. To get there take the Metro to its station called Campi Flegrei, or the Cumana train from Montesanto to Mostra d'Oltremare, then walk uphill to Via Terracina, past the towering modern stadium of Napoli F.C. The baths lie just east of the junction between Via Terracina and Via Marconi, and are visible from the street. Nearby, but invisible from the street, is a much restored brick-built tomb, in the form of a small temple, with neat pilasters along its outer walls. Some paving of the Roman highway is visible beside it.

The Roman traveller heading for Naples on the lower route passed through a 700m-long tunnel which Strabo attributes to the engineer Cocceius, beginning on Via Grotta Vecchia in the suburb called Fuorigrotta, and emerging at Piedigrotta close to the seafront promenade at Mergellina, a route followed at a lower level by modern road tunnels. Cocceius' tunnel, now the Crypta Neapolitana or Grotta Vecchia, hence the modern place-names Piedigrotta ('at the tunnel's foot') and Fuorigrotta ('outside the tunnel'), is mentioned by several Roman authors, among them Seneca who describes an uncomfortable journey through it in AD 63–5. To reach its eastern end, turn right on emerging from the newly restored magnificence of Napoli Mergellina train station into busy Via Piedigrotta, then, after passing below a bridge carrying the railway but before the entrance to one of the road tunnels, go leftwards into the quiet garden setting of the Parco Virgiliano. The vertical hillside is clothed in an attractive ivy coating. Recent EU funding has allowed the installation of closed-circuit television and information panels.

A winding ramp brings the visitor first to the classical-style tomb of the nineteenth-century poet Giacomo Leopardi, carried off at the age of 39 by cholera, then to a squat tomb on a strikingly lofty plinth, next to the entrance to the Roman tunnel (*26*). This was long identified as the burial place of the poet Virgil who we are told was buried in 19 BC beside the coastal road, between the first and second milestones westwards from Naples. The visible tomb occupied a very conspicuous position for users of the tunnel, and had involved much shaping of the soft volcanic rock. (Access is via a long narrow stairway set against the hillside.) The tomb was an obligatory halt for travellers through the ages, who included Dante, Petrarch and Boccaccio, the young Mozart with his father, and the Grand Tourists of the eighteenth and nineteenth centuries. Sprigs from a myrtle bush beside the tomb, traditionally planted by Petrarch himself, became a must-have souvenir, so much so that by the early nineteenth century the bush had been entirely defoliated.

However, Virgil's tomb needs to be sought elsewhere, since the visible structure is in fact a *columbarium* of the early first century AD, containing niches for ten or more ash-urns. Much robbed of its original *opus reticulatum* cladding, it was restored in 1930 on the occasion of the 2000th anniversary of the Virgil's birth. Just beyond is the eastern entrance to the tunnel itself; there is no access currently, on safety grounds, but the visitor has a view along its length to the western exit. An adjacent aqueduct tunnel carried the Aqua Augusta on its parallel route from Neapolis to Puteoli and beyond.

In Roman times this stretch of coast was in open country, and doubtless seaside villas fringed the shore, one indeed likely to have belonged to Virgil, where he is supposed to have composed many of his finest works and where

26 Naples, the 'Tomb of Virgil' on its lofty plinth, beside the eastern entrance to the Grotta Neapolitana

he was buried. Another villa is mentioned by the philosopher Philostratus writing in the later second century:

> I was staying outside the wall [of Neapolis] in a suburb facing on to the sea, in which there was a portico open to the west wind, built on four, I think, or even five terraces, looking out on the Tyrrhenian Sea. It was decked out with all the marbles which luxury applauds, but it was particularly splendid by reason of the panel-paintings set in the walls, which I thought had been collected with discernment.

The topographical description suggests that the villa was set on the cliffs hereabouts.

8. Naples

Naples is nowadays the chief city on the Bay, a metropolis of nearly three million people lying in the shadow of Vesuvius. Its rise in the Late Empire and after corresponded with the decline of Puteoli. Urban sprawl has long since swallowed up areas that were countryside in Roman times. Its many grand buildings reflect a long-time status as the capital city of a kingdom.

In origin this was a Greek settlement, a daughter colony of Cumae, established in the seventh century BC on the promontory of Parthenope, now Pizzofalcone, above the famous fishermen's quarter of Santa Lucia. The settlement was subsequently transferred eastwards to the present location, which became known as the New Town (in Greek, *Nea Polis*). In Roman times the town of Neapolis maintained a particularly Greek character, nourished by the emperors and sustained by its own population. It was a favoured residence of philosophers, poets and artists and was a place of retirement for wealthy Romans.

Roman masonry structures on the promontory of Pizzofalcone front on to the island of Megaris (now Megaride), the latter now topped by the Castel dell'Ovo. Lucullus owned a villa here, from which columns were re-used in the castle's structure. It was at this villa that Romulus Augustulus, the last emperor of Rome in AD 475–76, sat out the remaining years of his life.

The modern visitor is likely to begin at the National Archaeological Museum; there is a good bookshop, and a café in one of the courtyards.

Unfortunately some of the exhibition galleries close by rotation in the busiest summer months; visits to them at fixed times may be announced at the entrance. The museum is situated in the Piazza Museo Nazionale, close to the Via Cavour metro station, one stop along Line 2 from the main railway station in Piazza Garibaldi, and now connected to the museum itself by an underground walkway. (Hours: 9.00–19.30; closed Tuesdays. Soon the visitor will be able to reach a new station called 'Museo' directly from Piazza Garibaldi on Line 1, currently under construction.)

Built as royal stables and later the site of the city's university, the building opened as the Real Museo Borbonico in 1816–18. Plaques and statues to the Neapolitan kings still adorn the stairways. The Museum's contents were originally more wide-ranging, and included an extensive library and many paintings later transferred to the former royal palace at Capodimonte.

The Museum holds stupendous collections of antiquities garnered over the centuries chiefly from Pompeii and Herculaneum but also from Cuma, Pozzuoli, Baia, Castellammare and Capri, which found their way into the royal collection of the Bourbon kings. Many were housed originally in their palace at Portici (below, p. 96). Exhibits include bronze statuary from the poolside of the Villa of the Papyri at Herculaneum and some of the carbonised papyrus rolls which gave that villa its modern name (below, p. 109). Paintings cut from the walls of Pompeii, Herculaneum and Stabiae include scenes from Greek and Roman mythology, portraits of house owners, still-lifes and garden scenes, and the famous depiction of the riot in the amphitheatre at Pompeii (below, p. 131). Gladiators' helmets found in the portico of its theatre are highlighted. A 'secret room' houses phallic symbols and other erotic paraphernalia once considered too shocking for unrestricted public access. Numerous fine mosaics include the much restored scene from the House of the Faun at Pompeii depicting Alexander the Great confronting King Darius of the Persians in battle (below p. 138). There are displays on daily life, with bronzeware from the kitchen and for the banquet. A large-scale model of the excavations at Pompeii – made in 1861–79 out of wood, cork and paper – preserves some details of structures and wall-paintings long since disintegrated on site.

In addition, the Museum houses the Neapolitan royal collection of sculpture which King Charles of Bourbon inherited from his mother, Elisabetta Farnese, and which was transferred to Naples from the Palazzo Farnese in Rome by his son Ferdinand in 1787. The pieces include the gigantic Farnese Bull and the Farnese Hercules – both from the Baths of Caracalla in Rome – and a Roman copy of the Athenian tyrannicides Harmodius and Aristogeiton from Hadrian's villa at Tivoli. There are many busts and statues of Roman emperors in marble and bronze, substantial epigraphic and numismatic collections, and some Egyptian antiquities in the basement. The courtyards showcase inscriptions on altars, funerary monuments and milestones. On the floor of the main upper hall, originally the library, is a meridian line, laid in 1790–93.

Neapolis, like the other Roman towns on the Bay, was a walled city lying directly on the coast, with harbourworks in front, parts of which (now

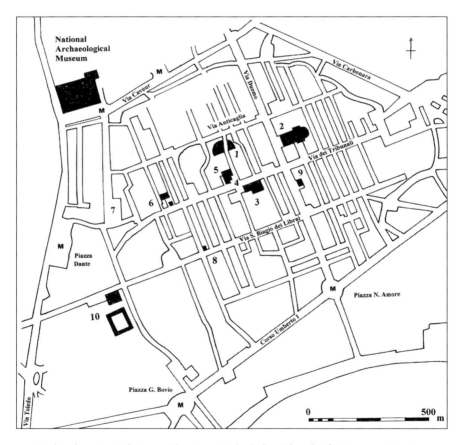

27 Naples, the principal sites: 1. Theatre; 2. Cathedral; 3. Church of S. Lorenzo Maggiore; 4. Piazza Gaetano; 5. Church of S. Paolo Maggiore; 6. Church of S. Maria della Pietrasanta; 7. Piazza Bellini; 8. Statue of River Nile; 9. Vico Carminiello ai Mannesi; 10. Church and cloister of S. Chiara. M = metro station

some distance inland) are being explored during extensions to the city's metro system (*27*). Excavation below Piazza N. Amore (station Duomo) revealed a complex centred on a temple graced with statues of the imperial family. Inscribed marble panels listed victors in games instituted in AD 2 by Augustus. To the south-west, three ships found below Piazza Municipio (station Municipio), two perhaps sunk deliberately and the third still carrying its cargo, are important for the study of shipbuilding techniques and trading patterns. Most recently, sculptured reliefs showing a religious procession have been brought to light in Piazza G. Bovio (station Università), re-used in sixth-century Byzantine fortifications. Some of the finds have been placed on view in a basement exhibition, 'Stazione Neapolis', below the Archaeological Museum, the modern design in stark contrast to the often antiquated displays in the galleries above.

The street layout of Graeco-Roman Neapolis is readily appreciated on a modern map or from an aerial photograph (*27*). The north–south axes (or *cardines*) are on the alignment of Via Duomo and the many parallel streets, the east–west axes (or *decumani*) on the alignment of Via dei Tribunali and Via San Biagio dei Librai (*28*), the whole bounded, as discoveries of lengths of the Graeco-Roman walls have demonstrated, on the north by Via Luigi Settembrini (just south of Via Cavour), on the west by Via Santa Maria di Costantinopoli and, as it may be, Via Mezzocannone (to the east of Via Toledo), on the south by Corso Umberto I and on the east by Via S. Giovanni a Carbonara. The Archaeological Museum lies just beyond the north-western corner of the ancient town, and Piazza Garibaldi, fronting the Napoli Centrale railway station, a short distance to the east. The walls are visible in a number of places, including at Piazza Bellini.

Our knowledge of public and private buildings, all traces of which at first sight later structures seem to have obliterated, is always increasing. As we shall see, it is often to Naples' churches that the visitor must go to see meaningful evidence of the Greek and Roman past, some of it revealed by wartime bombing in 1943.

The Forum lay south of Via dei Tribunali, and included the area of the small Piazza S. Gaetano. Its overall extent is unknown, but it was flanked to the east by a market building (*macellum*), of which part was exposed during restoration work below the church of S. Lorenzo Maggiore. (Hours: weekdays 9.30–17.30; Sundays 9.30–13.30.) Access is from the cloister, where the visitor can view behind railings part of the marble-clad base of a circular fountain, which lay within a market building of the type exemplified by

28 Naples, Via S. Biagio dei Librai, on the alignment of a Graeco-Roman street

the *Serapeum* at Pozzuoli (above p. 73). Ranges of rooms on its south and east sides are reached by descending a stairway. The different levels reflect the original north-to-south slope of the ground hereabouts. Walling datable to the mid-first century AD, with later additions, stands remarkably to a height of about 2.5m, perserving shops, storerooms and offices. Next to an elaborate brick doorway (*29*) is a window once fitted with vertical iron bars, which has been interpreted as the town's municipal treasury. The splendid paving of a broad street can be followed down to a T-junction and then right to a covered fish market, with sloping stone slabs and facilities for running water. Some fine Greek walling can also be viewed. The whole area was later covered by silt and then cut into by medieval and later buildings. One floor of the adjacent museum is given over to finds from the site; displays set the excavations in the urban context of ancient Neapolis and of wider trading patterns. There is a model of the complex as restored and a helpful site plan.

Across the street, the church of S. Paolo Maggiore overlies a Roman temple to the Dioscuri (Castor and Pollux), which faced southwards onto the Forum. A length of walling with *opus reticulatum* facings is visible on the church's façade below its grand stairways. In the sixteenth century the architect Palladio gained artistic inspiration from the temple which survived as the shell of a medieval church till earthquakes brought it down. Two of the original columns are preserved in the much altered façade, and the bases of two more are placed in front. Napoli Sotterranea (entered from the left side of the church, at Piazza Gaetano 68), is one of two organisations in the city offering guided tours of the extensive underground water-supply system. (For the other, whose rendezvous point is Piazza Trieste e Trento

29 Naples, doorway on
north–south Roman street
below the church of
S. Lorenzo Maggiore

beside Teatro S. Carlo, see www.lanapolisotterranea.it.) To either side of the
entrance in Piazza Gaetano the visitor is greeted rather incongruously by
mannequins in Second World War uniforms, reflecting the re-use of the
tunnels in 1939–45 as air raid shelters, testified to by graffiti. The visitor
needs to be fit (there is a descent of close on 150 steps), slim and not be
claustrophobic to be able to navigate the cold and damp tunnels in order to
complete the itinerary, which is a fascinating experience.

A short distance away along Via dei Tribunali to the west, the twelfth-
century bell tower of the much older church of S. Maria Maggiore della
Pietrasanta incorporates column shafts, capitals and cornices from one or
more Roman buildings (*30*). Opposite is the dignified Cappella Pontano,
built in 1492 as a family chapel by the humanist scholar Giovanni Pontano,
and ornamented with Greek and Latin inscriptions he composed.

30 Naples, Roman
stonework built into the
bell-tower of S. Maria
della Pietrasanta

From a remark by the poet Statius – describing to his wife in the later first century AD the appeal of Neapolis as a desirable place of retirement after the bustle of Rome – we know that Naples had two theatres, side by side, one open to the sky and the other roofed (i.e. an *odeum*); both may overlie Greek predecessors. A segment of the perimeter wall of the larger theatre is visible on the south side of Via Anticaglia. The theatre was built under Augustus and restored in the Flavian period. Excavations have been in progress out of view from the street; a visit can be made courtesy of Napoli Sotterranea, beginning in Piazza Gaetano (see above), and more general access may be possible before too long. The brick arches spanning Via Anticaglia were part of buttressing added in the late second or early third centuries, in consequence of earth tremors, or the fear of them (*31*).

The theatre at Neapolis was patronised by the emperors. A comic play in Greek, written by the scholarly Emperor Claudius, was performed there in AD 42. In AD 64 it collapsed shortly after Nero had sung on stage. Seneca, writing in the early 60s AD to his friend Lucilius, commented that

> on the way to the house of Metronax, the theatre of the Neapolitans must be passed. The building is absolutely full up, and much zeal is being expended on who is a good fluteplayer; even the Greek trumpeter and herald have an audience.

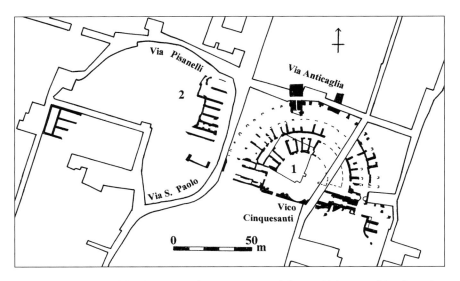

31 Naples, location of the theatres: 1. Theatre; 2. Covered theatre. (After Macchiaroli 1985)

A pronounced curvature of Via Pisanelli immediately to the west may, it is suggested, conceal the outer wall of the second, smaller theatre.

Further east, the cathedral begun in 1294 incorporates as a side-chapel on its north side, opposite the Treasury of S. Gennaro, a much earlier basilica dedicated to S. Restituta. Granite and marble column shafts from Roman buildings in the town are re-used here in the naves. From the far end of the left-hand nave, access is gained along narrow passageways to a complicated sequence of occupation on the same site over many centuries, partly under S. Restituta and partly under adjacent church buildings. Early Christian mosaics overlie Roman structures which in turn overlie Greek walls and a deeply rutted paved street. The right-hand route leads the visitor to a series of vaulted cisterns with *opus reticulatum* facings. The main site lies to the left, where the visitor can see part of a portico with a water channel and lead piping stamped with the maker's name, Aurelius Uticianus. At a higher level beyond, flooring of the Late Roman and Early Christian periods shows evidence of re-use of materials, including a fragment of a marble inscription. (Hours: weekdays, 9.00–12.00, 16.30–19.00; Sundays, 8.30–13.00.)

The wartime destruction of the church of S. Maria del Carmine (*32*) in Vico Carminiello ai Mannesi (off Via Duomo south of Via dei Tribunali) revealed baths and 18 rooms of an apartment building on at least two storeys; there is no access, but it is readily visible from the street. One room at the lower level was later converted into a temple to Mithras.

At the next major crossroads downhill, turn westwards along Via S. Biagio dei Librai (one of the Graeco-Roman city's *decumani*). A large reclining statue of the River Nile, dating perhaps to the second or third century AD, holding a brimming cornucopia and flanked by what remains of a crocodile, sits outdoors on a plinth in the Largo Corpo di Napoli, beside the church of S. Angelo a Nilo. The head is modern. Deriving from baths nearby, or from a temple of the Egyptian goddess Isis, the statue has been remarked upon by travellers and sketched by artists through the ages. The explanatory Latin inscription dates to 1734. Other Neapolitan churches, many overlying Early Christian basilicas, have architectural fragments built into them, or employ Roman columns. Excavation in the city regularly reveals Roman floors and walling. An amphitheatre, testified to in the documentary evidence, lay close to but within the walls of the city on its eastern flank, but not even its shape is preserved in the modern street layout.

In an area outside the city walls to the west, but which had become built up by the early centuries AD, a brick-built bath-house with swimming pool

32 Naples, Roman remains in Vico Carminiello ai Mannesi

was revealed in 1951–52 during repairs following wartime bombing, under the fourteenth-century convent of Santa Chiara, which is famed for the majolica-decorated columns in its cloister gardens (Via S. Chiara, off Via B. Croce, the westwards continuation of Via S. Biagio dei Librai). Some elements of the baths, in use from the first to the fourth centuries AD, have been laid out for viewing both indoors and outside under corrugated perspex covers (*33*) where they are accessed by walkways (Hours: weekdays 9.30–17.00; Sundays 9.30–13.30). The on-site museum has Roman material including a dedicatory slab to the deified Faustina, wife of Emperor Antoninus Pius; it had been built into the church and was found during restoration work. An inscribed lead pipe with the name Caecina Albinus, consul in the AD 360s, testifies to late Roman refurbishment of the heating system of the baths.

On the other, eastern side of the city, brick-faced concrete arches of the Aqua Augusta aqueduct (above, p. 33) survive as the Ponti Rossi ('Red Bridges', after the brick-coloured arches), in Via Ponti Rossi, on the south-east flank of the Capodimonte Hill and just north of the Tangenziale motorway. The aqueduct crosses the modern street close to a distinctive multi-storey apartment block with circular verandas.

Chance finds have revealed elements of the extensive cemeteries to be expected outside the city gates, most notably a series of intact rock-cut house-tombs deeply buried below Via dei Cristallini, north-east of the Archaeological Museum, each accessed in antiquity by steps from a vestibule. The tombs, not currently open to visitors except by special permit, were hollowed out in the third century BC, but continued in use into the Roman imperial period.

Catacombs, in use for Christian and other burials from at least the early third century AD onwards, are outside the scope of this guidebook, but the visitor can be directed to those of S. Gennaro (Via Capodimonte, 16), of S. Gaudioso (Via della Sanità, 124), of S. Severo (Piazzetta S. Severo a Capodimonte) and of S. Eufebio (beside the church of Immacolata Concezione in Piazza G. B.Vico).

33 Naples, Roman baths at the cloister of S. Chiara. (L. Keppie)

9. Herculaneum

We could easily suppose that coastal villas existed in Roman times along the shore south-eastwards from Naples, but little is known, the result perhaps of the inexorable expansion of the modern city. More significantly, urbanisation is beginning to impinge on the areas affected by ash falls and lava flows from Vesuvius (*34*).

The seventeenth and eighteenth centuries saw the construction of villas by wealthy Neapolitan families on a massive scale along the coast between the city and Torre Annunziata. As a result one stretch of road, between Ercolano and Torre del Greco, became known as the Miglio d'Oro (the Golden Mile). Over 120 of these *ville vesuviane* are attested; some can be seen from the Autostrada del Sole, or from the train. It was the owner of

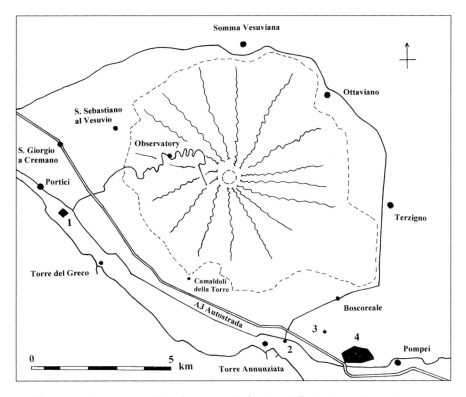

34 Vesuvius and environs: 1. Herculaneum; 2. Oplontis; 3.Villa Regina; 4. Pompeii

one such villa, the Prince d'Elbeuf, who in 1709–16 undertook the earliest excavations on the site of the theatre at Herculaneum. His own villa, which survives, occupies a splendid seafront position.

King Charles of Bourbon (reigned 1738–59), an indefatigable huntsman like his son and successor Ferdinand (1759–1825), began in 1738 the construction of a palace at Portici ('the Porticoes'), a name claimed as deriving from a supposed Portico of Hercules. Wide swathes of territory were designated as deer parks, and the kings' hunting expeditions ranged far to the south and inland to the foothills of the Appennines. 'The king [Ferdinand] is away hunting, the Queen is pregnant, things couldn't be going better', as Goethe observed on his arrival in Naples in February 1787. The Palace's location afforded the King and Queen easy visiting of the newly found site of Herculaneum which fell within royal property, and even while the palace at Portici was being built, a special wing was constructed to house the spectacular finds being discovered nearby.

A visit to Herculaneum is often considered a more satisfying experience than Pompeii and should perhaps be tackled first. The compactness of the exposed remains will prove less exhausting, the survival to roof level of the houses affords a better understanding of their original form, and the presence of the modern Neapolitan suburb of Ercolano (formerly known as Resina), closely hemming in the archaeological site on two sides, emphasises the continuity of life on the Bay, as well as the depth of coverage by the volcanic deposits which, unlike at Pompeii, preserved wooden furnishings and fitments in a carbonised state.

From the Circumvesuviana railway station Ercolano Scavi, walk directly downhill on Via IV Novembre until the monumental site-entrance comes into view straight ahead. By car, use the Ercolano exit from the A3 Autostrada. A spacious modern reception-building is now functioning, with disabled toilets and an education facility. Further developments are in progress nearby, including a car and bus park. (Hours: April – October 8.30–19.30; November – March 8.30–17.00. Closed 1 January, 1 May, 25 December.)

A period of at least three hours should be allowed for a basic itinerary. No refreshments are currently available once the turnstile is passed, but a convenient pizzeria and some bars lie immediately opposite the entrance. The presence of the much visited site has had limited economic impact, except very localised, on the town's economy; within 50m of the entrance, life remains largely unaffected. However, there is a new museum

1 Vesuvius, seen from the Marina Piccola, Sorrento. (L. Keppie)

2 Pompeii, excavation of the Temple of Isis, 1765, as depicted by Pietro Fabris in Sir William Hamilton, *Campi Phlegraei, Observations on the Volcanos of the Two Sicilies*. (Glasgow University Library)

3 Miseno, Shrine of the *Augustales*

4 Baia, 'Temple of Venus'

5 Pozzuoli, subterranean compartments below the amphitheatre

6 Gaiola, looking eastwards along the Grotta di Seiano. The supporting arches were added in Bourbon times

7 Posillipo, Palace of the Spirits

8 Herculaneum, wall-painting in the Seat of the *Augustales*

9 Herculaneum, fountainhead on the *decumanus maximus*. (L. Keppie)

10 Herculaneum, *Triclinium* in the House of Neptune and Amphitrite, with the eponymous wall–mosaic and sunken water-feature in front

11 Herculaneum, House of the Trellis

12 Boscoreale, reconstructed *villa rustica* at Villa Regina

13 Pompeii, the Forum, looking north towards the *Capitolium*

14 Pompeii, Temple of Apollo

15 Pompeii, Bakery of Popidius Priscus

16 Pompeii, painted election notices on the Via dell'Abbondanza. (L. Keppie)

17 Pompeii, counter at the Bar of Vetutius Placidus

18 Pompeii, garden of the House of 'Loreius Tiburtinus', looking along the north–south water channel

19 Pompeii, house-tombs outside the Nuceria Gate

20 Pompeii, arena of the amphitheatre. (L. Keppie)

21 Pompeii, the theatre

22 Sorrento, foundations offshore in front of the Hotel Bellevue Syrene

23 Capo di Sorrento, access-bridge to the villa (which lies to the left), looking eastwards past Sorrento towards Punta Scutolo. (L. Keppie)

24 The Anglo-American Project, work in progress near the Herculaneum Gate, 2004.

(www.museomav.com) at Via IV Novembre 44, offering a virtual tour, with a bookshop and exhibition spaces.

The historian Sisenna, writing in the early first century BC, described Herculaneum as 'a fortified city with modest walls on an eminence rising from the sea, between two rivers.' This can never be the modern visitor's perception; the shoreline, moved forward again by flowing lava after an eruption in 1631, now lies some 400m further out.

Excavation by means of tunnels began in earnest in 1738 (above, p. 48), which over the following decades revealed the theatre, the Villa of the Papyri, the basilica and palaestra, as well as a cemetery, mostly now off-limits to the modern visitor (35). From 1825 and again from 1927 onwards excavation was by large-scale removal of the overburden from ground level. Only part of the site has been cleared, and it is easy to see why (36). The labour of digging through the now solidified volcanic deposit (which can be seen in profile round much of the site's perimeter) and the potentially high cost of compensation and the resettlement of residents living on top are major obstacles. The visitor's gaze is likely to focus on the modern housing, but substantial areas to the west, south and east lie below market gardens. Funding

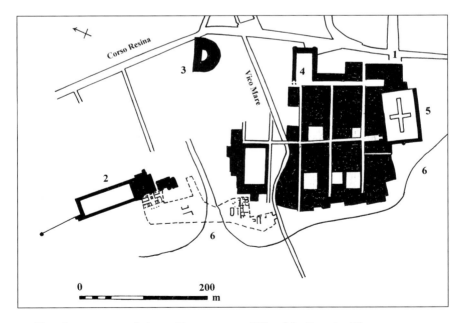

35 Herculaneum, general plan: 1. Site entrance; 2. Villa of the Papyri; 3. Theatre; 4. *Augusteum*; 5. Palaestra; 6. River course; - - - Limit of area excavated 1996–98

from the Packard Humanities Institute, in conjunction with the EU Regional Development Fund, the Region of Campania, the Comune of Ercolano and the British School at Rome (cf. above, p. 16), has enabled demolition of derelict buildings which long towered over the north-west corner of the site. Wholesale consolidation is currently underway along the site's northern side. Though this means that part of the town's *decumanus maximus* is currently out of bounds to visitors on safety grounds (*36*), the longer-terms benefits are clear. (For convenience I adhere here to the standard orientation, where the side facing the shore is designated south and the volcano north.)

Whereas our knowledge of the precise extent of Pompeii is known, in that it is enclosed by visible stone walls, we remain uncertain of the overall size of Herculaneum, except that it was defined on either side by river courses (*35*). Several blocks (*insulae*) of housing orientated on the seafront are exposed, bounded on the east by a palaestra. The theatre lies some 150m to the north-west on the same street-grid. Unlike at Pompeii (below, p. 121), where streets have names given by the excavators, at Herculaneum a sequence of numbered north–south *cardines* and east–west *decumani* is employed, which the visitor will find marked on information posts at street corners.

The long curving access ramp, in part arched over the Roman town, allows fine vistas of it and, near the bottom, of the ancient sea frontage. An information board and plan set the scene, and the volcano lies what seems only a short distance behind. Standing at the information board and facing northwards towards Vesuvius, one can see directly into the arcades which once fronted on to the Bay, to either side of a stair leading to the foreshore. They may have served as boat sheds or for fishermen's gear. It was here that the skeletons of 300 people, including babies and children, were found, sheltering from the effects of the volcano's eruption (above, p. 45). Here too lay an armed soldier. Finds included a doctor's portable medical kit. Upturned on the beach was a wooden boat.

From the information panel the visitor can look directly across to seafront houses, in particular the House of the Inn and the House of the Stags, whose owners had developed gardens, terraces and porticoes to take advantage of the view. Immediately above the beach, directly in front of the board, are remnants of two small temples, one possibly dedicated to Venus. Further to the right is a terrace topped by a statue and funerary altar (below, p. 107), and the dramatically positioned Suburban Baths. Herculaneum has the air of a quiet residential seaside town, but we see only a part of it, lacking many public buildings and temples.

36 Herculaneum, view westwards along the *decumanus maximus*, with stabilisation work in progress

A newly installed bridge brings the visitor directly on to one of the main north–south streets (*Cardo III*). On the left is a series of partially exposed houses, including the House of Argus with its grandly columned portico. On the right is the porticoed garden of the House of the Inn (from its original identification, now discredited). The ancient visitor would have entered

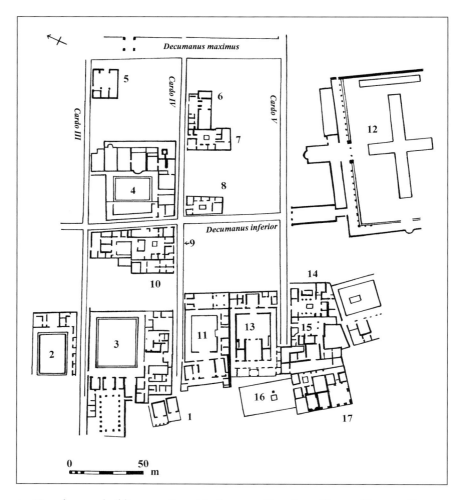

37 Herculaneum, buildings mentioned in the text: 1. Temples; 2. House of Argus; 3. House of the Inn; 4. Central Baths; 5. Seat of the *Augustales*; 6. House of the Beautiful Courtyard; 7. House of Neptune and Amphitrite; 8. Samnite House; 9. House of the Wooden Partition; 10. House of the Trellis; 11. House of the Mosaic *Atrium*; 12. Palaestra; 13. House of the Stags; 14. House of the Relief of Telephus; 15. House of the Gem; 16. Terrace; 17. Suburban Baths

the house from *Cardo IV*, passing a private bath-suite on the right of the entrance, before reaching the large upper courtyard, from which he could pass through a reception room, to a smaller portico on the lower terrace.

The Central Baths, which occupied the complete width of the block between *Cardo III* and *Cardo IV*, were laid out in the later first century BC; they were divided in the normal way into separate men's and women's facilities (*38*). The men entered from *Cardo III* along a narrow corridor leading to the *frigidarium* with a marble basin in the apse; a circular cold plunge bath to one side was painted in a marine blue, with sea creatures on the underside of its domed ceiling. The mosaic floor of the *tepidarium* beyond was decorated with a triton and dolphins. The rooms had fine stuccoed ceilings and were fitted with masonry seats and shelves for depositing clothes. The *caldarium* had a raised oblong bath at one end, and marble seats;

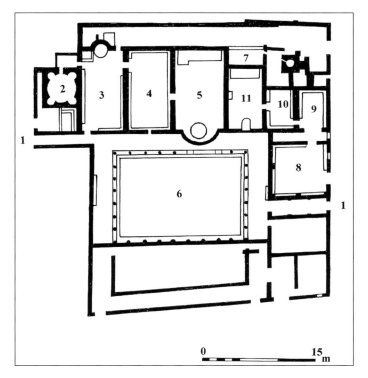

38 Herculaneum, the Central Baths: Men's suite, 1. Entrance; 2. Circular cold bath; 3. *Apodyterium*; 4. *Tepidarium*; 5. *Caldarium*; 6. Palaestra; 7. *Praefurnium*. Women's suite, 8. Vestibule; 9. *Apodyterium;* 10. *Tepidarium;* 11. *Caldarium*. (After Guidobaldi 2006)

at the other end, only the masonry plinth of a circular basin survives. The curving apse is reflected in the shape of the external wall fronting on to an exercise courtyard. The women's suite, on a much smaller scale except for a large vestibule, was entered separately from *Cardo IV*. The mosaic floor of its a*podyterium* was decorated with marine animals (like the *tepidarium* of the men's rooms) and its *tepidarium* with a fine geometric design. The *caldarium*, through the wall from the men's *caldarium*, similarly had a raised hot bath at one end backing on to the furnace room which served both suites. There was a porticoed courtyard for exercise, access to which was possible only from the men's side.

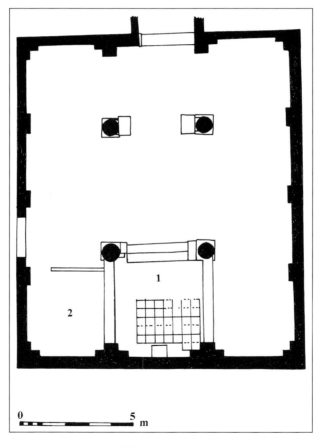

39 Herculaneum, Seat of the *Augustales*: 1. Shrine; 2. Caretaker's room. (After Guadagno 1983)

The modern visitor can now head uphill on *Cardo III* to arrive at the north-western corner of the site (top left when seen from the information board). Below the high banking of solidified volcanic deposit was the Seat of the *Augustales* (*39*), whose interiors were lavishly decorated with wall-paintings featuring well known mythological figures including the legendary hero Hercules, after whom the town was named (*colour plate 8*). The roof of the hall was supported on columns, and in a second phase a walled shrine was created against its south wall, accessed by a couple of steps. A marble inscription, now set at eye level into an internal wall on the building's north side, reports a formal meal given during Augustus' reign on the inauguration day, by the brothers A. Lucius Proculus and A. Lucius Julianus, to the decurions of the town and to their fellow *Augustales*. Behind a flimsy partition a skeleton was found, which is suggested as of the caretaker; he remained during the eruption lying on his simple bed.

In the area beyond, i.e. northwards, concealed below the volcanic deposits, lay a major public building, which some identify as an *Augusteum*, a precinct dedicated to Augustus and his imperial successors. It was ornamented with statues to emperors of the Julio-Claudian dynasty, and its grand entrances were marked by brick-built archways, one of which, lying within the visible excavated area, was originally topped by a bronze statuary group of charioteer and horses. Across the street, westwards, was a portico which may have been part of a basilica (law court), explored in the eighteenth century but now hidden from view. The portico was adorned with statues of the senator Marcus Nonius Balbus (below, p. 107) and members of his family, who had paid for its construction.

Next it is as well to continue, if permitted by works in progress, along the town's main east–west street (*decumanus maximus*), i.e. along the northern limit of the exposed site (*36*), past a number of shops and food outlets, noticing the carbonised woodwork. One such establishment was called *Ad Cucumas* ('At the Jugs'), the name emblazoned on the street-frontage together with four glass jars and the prices for a drink from them. The numerous bars and snack-shops (sometimes termed *thermopolia*) are a feature of the town, as at Pompeii, each with a counter enclosing large terracotta urns (*dolia*) in which food and drink were kept handy for sale to customers. It was evidently easier to get lunch in ancient Herculaneum than it has often been inside the modern site. At intervals along the street were fountains, with attractive sculptured fountainheads (*colour plate 9*).

The city-blocks between this street and the parallel east–west *decumanus inferior*, lower down the slope towards the sea, contain many of the most visited houses, for example the House of the Beautiful Courtyard near the top of *Cardo IV*, with its enclosed central courtyard and stairway to an upper floor. A current display here features three of the skeletons from the seafront arcades, and explanatory panels. The adjacent House of Neptune and Amphitrite contains, in a little courtyard at the back, an open-air dining area with a central water-feature. Decoration on the walls creates the effect of a natural grotto, especially one wall with the mosaic which gives the house its modern name, showing the god Neptune and his sea-nymph wife (*colour plate 10*). To one side of the entrance to this house was a wine shop, perhaps operated by a freedman of the unknown owners, where amphorae have been imaginatively replaced on replicated racking.

At the bottom corner of the same block is the Samnite House, one of the oldest dwellings in the town; some of its original wall-paintings in the 'First Style' near the entrance are dated to the second century BC. Here the visitor, if viewing the house from the street – it is currently inaccessible – should raise his eyes to the remarkable *loggia* which might seem to belong more naturally in a much later age.

On the other side of *Cardo IV*, a little further downhill, is the House of the Wooden Partition; the original shuttering, retained in situ, separates the *atrium* from the reception room beyond. The adjacent House of the Trellis (*colour plate 11*), with its upper storey extended over the pavement, has been restored to highlight its timber-framed, low-cost method of construction (*opus craticium*); the internal partitioning and surviving wooden furnishings have suggested that this was a boarding house.

Near the bottom end of *Cardo IV* was the House of the Mosaic Atrium with its undulating floor, and a reception room beyond. It is currently closed on safety grounds, but the *atrium* itself is visible from the street. The house appears at first sight a quite modest dwelling, but to one side was a large peristyle, and beyond, towards the sea, a grand *triclinium*, leading to a terrace flanked by square belvederes.

The eastern end of town was dominated by the palaestra (*40*), a spacious gymnasium and exercise area of the type we shall see again at Pompeii, entered by a corridor from *Cardo V*. A hall on its western side could have housed a large statue. Built during Augustus' reign, there were porticoes on three of its sides, and a two-storey arcade on the fourth, below the modern access ramp. Tunnels driven horizontally through the overburden

40 Herculaneum, portico of the Palaestra

have exposed a cruciform swimming pool at its centre, topped by a bronze fountain in the form of a five-headed serpent.

Turning seawards again, the visitor can walk southwards along *Cardo V* towards the narrow Marine Gate. Nearer the seafront, the houses were again larger and more opulent, among them the House of the Stags (on the right of *Cardo V*, going downhill). The modest entrance and simple *atrium* belie the grandeur of what lay beyond, with a *triclinium* looking seawards on to a garden decorated with the marble statues which give the house its modern name (*41*). Beyond was a large room, perhaps a second, larger *triclinium* or a grand salon, which faced both the garden and a small covered pergola, which is one of the first structures the visitor's eye will light on, as seen from the information board on the main access ramp (*42*). The owner enjoyed an enviable view of the Bay from his sun terrace.

41 Herculaneum, pergola and sun terrace of the House of the Stags

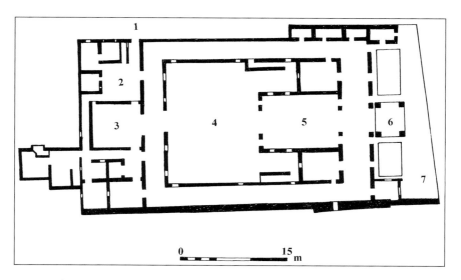

42 Herculaneum, House of the Stags: 1. Entrance; 2. *Atrium*; 3. *Triclinium*; 4. Garden;
5. Grand Salon; 6. Pergola; 7. Sun terrace. (After Guidobaldi 2006)

On the east side of the same street was the House of the Relief of Telephus, with its side-garden and lower-level peristyle facing towards the water course which originally flanked the town on its eastern side; the visitor descending the main access ramp will have noticed on the right its dramatic three-storey façade. Its *atrium* is fitted up with copies of circular marble discs called *oscilla*, carved with Dionysiac scenes, suspended between the columns. The House of the Gem in front overlooked the Suburban Baths; in a toilet opening off the *atrium* was a graffito stating that Apollinaris, Emperor Titus' doctor, 'had a good crap here', a somewhat bizarre revelation.

From the Marine Gate steps led down to the Suburban Baths lodged against the sea frontage. The eye will be immediately caught by a funerary altar commemorating Marcus Nonius Balbus, senatorial proconsul of Crete and Cyrenaica under Augustus, and at that time the town's most distinguished resident (*43*). The inscription records that his body was cremated on this spot, his ashes collected and deposited here in an urn. The smaller base nearby is topped by a cast of a newly restored marble statue of Balbus in military dress, found in fragments some distance away on the beach, presumably swept there by the pyroclastic surges. No visitor to the baths in antiquity could remain unaware of Balbus' importance. He and his family owned, it is suggested, the houses above, as well as the baths in front.

The baths, if accessible to visitors (they are often closed due to water-penetration and structural weakness), are an eye-opener, being completely intact to ceiling level, with all their mosaic floors, stuccoed walls, ceiling decoration, internal fittings and heating systems in situ, providing valuable technical details on the workings of such an establishment (*44*). Built under Augustus, the baths were reconstructed only a few years before AD 79. From the terrace, wooden steps led downwards into an *atrium*-court dramatically lighted from above, then to a carefully planned complex of rooms, designed to maximise the use of restricted space. Unlike most Roman baths this complex was not distinguished by domes or barrel vaulting above the heated rooms, which were instead lit by glazed skylights and by picture windows on to the sea. The views from the houses above were thus unimpeded.

The *atrium* led to a large *frigidarium* with a square cold bath opening off it, then sideways through a hinged wooden door into the *tepidarium*. Next the bather could turn right (westwards) into the *caldarium* with a small circular hot bath against the outer wall, or left (eastwards) to a rectangular heated swimming pool with a circular sauna room beyond. In AD 79 the hot ashy flows from the volcano burst into the *caldarium* through its outer window,

43 Herculaneum, funerary altar and statue of M. Nonius Balbus on terrace leading to the Suburban Baths

lifting a circular basin from its pedestal, which ended up against the far wall. Some fragments of the window glass fell into the bowl, and were embedded in the solidified deposit. The basin itself has been put back in its original position. There was also a circular sauna-room (*laconicum*). Floors were neatly laid with white marble squares. There was no separate women's section.

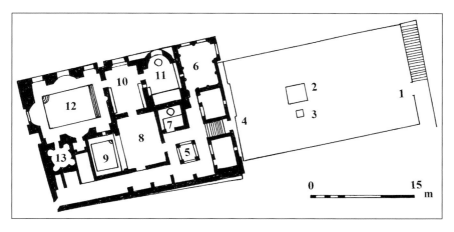

44 Herculaneum, the Suburban Baths: 1. Access to terrace; 2. Funerary altar of Nonius Balbus; 3. Statue of Nonius Balbus; 4. Entrance to baths; 5. *Atrium;* 6. Sun lounge; 7. *Praefurnium*; 8. *Frigidarium*; 9. Cold pool; 10. *Tepidarium*; 11. *Caldarium*; 12. Hot pool; 13. Sauna (After Guidobaldi 2006).

The visitor, if he has by now taken his fill of the site as a whole, can walk across a low bridge over the ancient shoreline, exiting up a stairway to emerge near the modern building long meant to serve as a museum, but which has never opened.

Immediately west of the town, and separated from it in antiquity by one of the river courses to which ancient authors refer, lay a palatial villa, known from discoveries made there in the eighteenth century as the Villa of the Papyri. Explored by tunnelling in 1750–61, a careful ground-plan was made while work was in progress by the Swiss engineer Karl Weber (45). Galley slaves were employed to drive the tunnels through the rock-hard deposits. Statues and sculptures decorating its rooms and its fish ponds were immediately removed to the nearby museum at Portici, and later to the Archaeological Museum in Naples (above, p. 85). Recent exploration (see below) has shown that there were a number of terraces which the original plan did not indicate. By AD 79, the villa had evolved from a rectangular house laid out in perhaps 60–40 BC, between the Neapolis-Herculaneum road and the shore, with its main focus towards the latter. There was a small peristyle garden on its north-east side, with a narrow central pool, and a service wing with baths. In a small room equipped with ceiling-high wooden cabinets, the tunnellers found hundreds of papyrus rolls, especially works in Greek of the Epicurean philosopher Philodemus who lived in the first century BC. Other rolls lay scattered on the floors, as though a hurried attempt had been made in AD 79 to rescue them as the eruption developed. The work of unrolling and deciphering the nearly 2000 papyri continues at the National Library in Naples, aided by ever more sophisticated text-imaging techniques being used by an international team.

Later the villa was extended north-westwards over a further distance of 150m, by the construction of an elongated peristyle with matching central pool. From here a terrace led to a belvedere and we can assume gardens to the rear. Nearly 100 statues in marble and bronze were recovered; the latter including deer, male athletes and draped girl 'dancers', enjoy a prominent place in the Archaeological Museum at Naples, together with wall-paintings detached from the walls. Many of the statues were originally set along the edges of the pool and between the columns of the peristyle.

The villa itself may at one time have been the property of L. Calpurnius Piso Caesoninus, Caesar's father-in-law (one of a number of possible owners; the list has grown in recent years), a known patron of the philosopher Philodemus; but who owned it in AD 79 is unknown. Though the villa looms large in any modern account of Romans on the Bay, it is salutary to remember that no ancient author mentions it.

As the site of the villa was not overtopped by modern buildings but by market gardens, gargantuan efforts were expensively made in 1996–98 to excavate down to it through the layers of volcanic deposits, to the extent that access may be gained to a limited range of rooms on its seaward side. (Guided tours at fixed times, by prior internet booking on www.arethusanet.it; but ask for availability at the on-site kiosk at the foot of the access ramp.) The visitor to the villa crosses a modern lane, the Vico Mare,

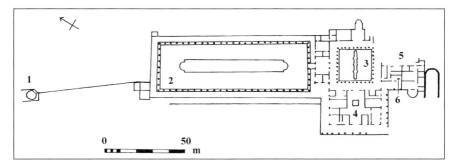

45 Villa of the Papyri: 1. Belvedere; 2. Large peristyle; 3. Small peristyle; 4. *Atrium*; 5. Baths; 6. Library. (After Parslow 1995)

46 Herculaneum, canyon created by excavations 1996–98, looking westwards past the lofty bath building towards rooms of the Villa of the Papyri, now topped by protective roofing. (L. Keppie)

from the administration building and toilet block, into the canyon created by the excavations, past a seafront house and, beyond it, a baths suite where a free-standing lofty building housed a heated swimming pool, apsed at one end (*46*). In a flanking courtyard were found a small boat and a now disintegrating horse skeleton, poorly protected under a glass and metal cover. A useful information panel relates the discoveries to the layout of the town as a whole.

The new excavations intruded into rooms flanking the *atrium* of the villa, revealing their mosaic floors; but the porticoes and the gardens remain out of view. Water penetration, kept at bay by pumps, restricts visits. Recently a well preserved wooden and ivory throne, decorated with scenes from the cult of Attis, a youthful Anatolian god symbolising rebirth and the afterlife, was found during remedial work. The design and ground plan of the J. Paul Getty Museum of Ancient Sculpture in Malibu, California, are closely based on this villa. Copies of many of the original marble and bronze statues stand in its garden spaces.

Retracing his steps up the ramp to the main site-entrance, the visitor may choose to turn left (north-westwards) along Corso Resina to pay homage at the site of the Roman theatre, revealed by tunnelling in the eighteenth century, which nowadays can be visited only by a special permit obtained in advance. There is a fine inscribed panel above the nineteenth-century access door.

Many visitors recorded their impressions (see above, p. 48). At one time there were several means of entering, eventually reduced to one. The ever critical Henry Coxe observed in 1815 that

> The traveller should know that the officious cicerone who stands at this entrance should not be regarded: the money paid here might as well be thrown into the street; his curiosity will only be wearied with a perpetual sameness; he will be dragged up and down through damp, cold passages, without light or fresh air.

The theatre at Herculaneum was built of stone from the ground up in the Augustan period, unlike the theatre at Pompeii which was partly set against a natural slope. It was of the standard Roman form, with a semicircular auditorium fronted by a built stage-frontage to the full height. The visitor must don protective headgear before descending steps cut in the volcanic deposits to the top of the seating, then downwards via the original tiers to the stage. At either end of the stage-structure are inscriptions naming benefactors. The arcaded exterior was graced on several levels by bronze and marble statues of Nonius Balbus and others, which are now at the Naples Archaeological Museum.

Continuing further along the modern street in the same direction, i.e. north-westwards towards Naples, the visitor will presently arrive at the Royal Palace of Portici (above p. 96), now occupied by the agriculture faculty of the University of Naples, and currently undergoing extensive restoration. Appropriately the botanical evidence from Roman ships found in the harbour of Neapolis (above, p. 87) is being analysed here. A small part of the once extensive grounds and gardens remains amid modern housing.

Walking the other way (south-eastwards) from the site entrance, the visitor will quickly reach a number of the eighteenth-century *ville vesuviane*; several have been newly restored, and many others survive. Campolieto, a villa built for Luzio di Sangro, Duke of Casacalenda between 1755 and 1775, with its circular portico-belvedere facing towards the sea, can be visited on a regular basis. Occasionally the villa houses welcome exhibitions of archaeological material from Herculaneum. Another villa, formerly Villa Ravone and now renamed Villa Maiuri in honour of the famous archaeologist (in Via Quattro Orologi, south-east of the archaeological site) has recently become the permanent home of the International Centre for the Study of Herculaneum.

10. Vesuvius

An ascent to the crater of Vesuvius has always been an essential element in any visit to the Bay (above, p. 49). A funicular railway built in 1880 was soon brought over by John Cook, son of the tour operator Thomas Cook (*12*). Much celebrated in local lore and inspiring the song '*Funiculì, Funiculà*', it fell victim to the eruption of 1944, to be replaced in 1953 by a chairlift, itself now dismantled. The modern visitor needs to make the final climb on foot, but a replacement chairlift is proposed. Nowadays a private company offering minibus tours to the summit has its office prominently near Ercolano train station. Taxis are also available. However, there is often little for the modern visitor to see once the crater's lip is reached, perhaps no more than a few wisps of smoke or steam in contrast to the fiery flows and pyrotechnics in the night sky which greeted the eighteenth-century traveller (*47*). The crater and its slopes are now included in an extensive Vesuvius National Park.

From the slopes and summit splendidly wide views over the Bay may be had. The original Vesuvius Observatory, built in 1841–47 (Via Osservatorio 14, on the approach road to the crater), now houses a museum of minerals and of the scientific instruments once used in monitoring seismic activity. (Hours: Saturday – Sunday 10.00–14.00. Schools and groups, Monday – Friday 9.00–14.00 by prior arrangement.) The volcano is now monitored from premises in Naples.

Roman villas have been found both north and south of Vesuvius along the coast, one indeed under the palace at Portici, and another on the nearby hill of Camaldoli della Torre, itself volcanic in origin, now topped by an eighteenth-century monastery. Somewhere along the coast, to one or other side of Herculaneum, was a seaside villa which Emperor Caligula had demolished: it was where his mother Agrippina the Elder had been confined under house arrest by his predecessor Tiberius.

At Villa Sora south-east of Torre del Greco a Roman villa, built around the middle of the first century BC and enlarged in the Julio-Claudian period, was excavated in Bourbon times and again in 1989, yielding wall-paintings

47 Visiting the crater of Vesuvius. (L. Keppie)

and garden sculpture. The rooms were terraced down to the sea. There is a proposal for an archaeological park, which will include consolidation of the surviving remains.

11. Oplontis

Further south and falling within the territory of ancient Pompeii is a major villa, generally identified as belonging to Poppaea, the wife of Nero between AD 62 and 65. Initially discovered, as were so many others, in the Bourbon era, it was comprehensively explored from 1964 onwards. To reach it from the Circumvesuviana Torre Azzunziata train station, subtitled 'Oplonti Villa di Poppea', turn left along Via Boselli past the welcoming Bar Vesuvio, then right into Via Sepolcri to its junction with Via Margherita di Savoia. By car, use the exit 'Torre Annunziata Sud' on Autostrada A3. Hours: April – October 8.30–19.30; November – March 8.30–17.00. Closed 1 January, 1 May and 25 December. A site-plan and illustrated booklet can be obtained with the tickets (48). The site, tightly hemmed in on all sides by the modern town of Torre Annunziata, was named Oplontis after a road-station known only from the Peutinger Table, a medieval copy of a Late Roman road map. Oplontis is a relatively new addition to the tourist itinerary, and it attracts disappointingly few visitors, with little positive impact on the economy of a run-down area.

The specific attribution to Poppaea, wife of Nero, results from the discovery of her name on an oil amphora found during the excavations. The senatorial family of the Poppaei owned a tileworks at or near Pompeii and other properties round the Bay, which could have passed to the well-known Poppaea by inheritance. After her death, the villa at Oplontis presumably became imperial property. At the time of the eruption in AD 79 it was unoccupied, lacking furnishings, tableware, kitchen utensils, and the smaller objets d'art that might have been expected to grace its numerous rooms; statues which may once have stood throughout the building were stored together for safekeeping. Evidently refurbishment was in progress.

The visitor approaches the villa from its landward side (*49*), passing through a formal garden planted with hibiscus; but it should be remembered that its primary orientation must have been out to sea, and facades there remain

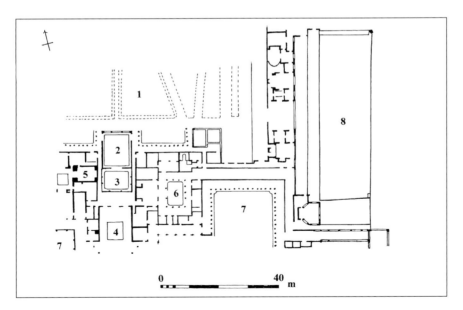

48 Oplontis, 'Villa of Poppaea': 1. Gardens; 2. Hall; 3. Enclosed garden; 4. *Atrium*; 5. Suite of baths; 6. Staff quarters; 7. Sea-facing peristyle; 8. Swimming pool. (After S. Jashemski in MacDougall 1987)

buried. The site has recently undergone a revamp of its drainage, lighting and other services. The excavated building is truncated to the north-west (the right, as viewed from the street); we could suppose a symmetrical arrangement, at least in its final form. Layers of pumice mixed with debris on the site's perimeter (*2*) are visible testimony to events on the fateful day in AD 79.

The columned façade which confronts the modern visitor is flanked by colonnades; they conceal a maze of rooms, at first sight seeming to lack a coherent plan. The original nucleus, dating to the mid-first century BC, consisted of an *atrium*, with a bath suite to one side and a peristyle on the other. Rooms ranged round the latter are modestly decorated, suggesting that these were, or had become, servants' quarters. In the Augustan period the complex was much enlarged, with the construction of the monumental facade and its flanking colonnades; the interiors were redecorated to the highest standards. Staircases suggest levels above and below the main complex. Additions to the original building on its eastern flank included an elongated swimming pool, now sometimes filled with rows of plastic chairs for concerts. The pool was found flanked by marble statues and small fountains in the form of centaurs. A series of colonnades doubtless formed

49 Oplontis, main façade of the 'Villa of Poppaea' (L. Keppie)

50 Oplontis, wall-painting in the *atrium* of the 'Villa of Poppaea', in the Second Style (mid first century BC), showing columns and false doorways

part of the façade overlooking the sea which, pushed back by volcanic debris, now lies 300m further away.

Attention has deservedly focused on the wall-paintings in the Second, Third and Fourth Styles, mosaics and stucco decoration, which taken together are of outstanding importance in our understanding of interior decoration in the Early Empire (50). The naturalistic scenes help us to envisage the botanical diversity of the surrounding landscape. Wooden window shutters are preserved in plaster, and ceiling-paintings have been restored in the corridor leading to the pool. An Oplontis Project, sponsored by the University of Texas at Austin, aims at comprehensive publication of the structures and the finds from them.

A second complex, found in 1974 barely 300m to the east during building work at the Scuola Media Parini, is not currently open to visitors, but to reach it one would continue downhill on Via Sepolcri, then left into Via G. Murat, past the school itself, to catch a tantalising glimpse of its two-tiered colonnade. The surviving walls are covered by a protective roof, but remain in limbo till funds can be found for their public presentation. This second building was not a seaside villa but, in part at least, a commercial establishment which processed the produce of the surrounding countryside. The owner lived on the upper floor, while various enterprises were carried on in the apartments below, which faced inwards towards a central courtyard. To the north, away from the sea, a series of small shop units opened on to a street, probably the road linking Herculaneum to Pompeii.

The likely Roman owner of this second complex is identifiable as L. Crassius Tertius, from the discovery of a seal-stamp mounted on a finger ring, the family name attested locally. Upstairs in the owner's apartments sat a fine bronze-decorated wooden chest with a complex locking system, which in AD 79 crashed through the floor to ground level; when found it was empty. If the 'Villa of Poppaea' was untenanted in AD 79, this second establishment was bustling with activity when disaster struck. More than 50 skeletons were found in one of its rooms, some wearing gold earrings and snake-bracelets, or carrying bags of coins. One skeleton, bearing a large amount of money and expensive jewellery, has been identified as Crassius Tertius himself. We can deduce – from the close proximity of the 'Villa of Poppaea' to other buildings – that the seafront here was thickly set with properties. An archaeological park to encompass the excavated remains was long ago proposed, but never implemented.

Other Roman properties have been located in or near Torre Annunziata, notably baths below the nineteenth-century Terme di Punta Oncino in the modern town, established to exploit the health-giving mineral waters. Offshore the small rocky islet of Rovigliano at the mouth of the River Sarno is the likely site of a shrine of Hercules. Later it was topped by a Benedictine monastery; walling in *opus reticulatum* survives in its foundations.

12. Boscoreale

To the north and east of Pompeii the Roman countryside was thickly set with *villae rusticae*, some known since Bourbon times, others revealed by chance in the 1890s and more recently. Sites are also known east of the volcano at Terzigno and to its north in the Comune of Somma Vesuviana where a villa, suggested as the house where Augustus died in AD 14, is being explored by a team from the University of Tokyo; its walls stand to a height of 9m.

Several of these *villae rusticae* lie in the modern Comune of Boscoreale (literally 'the Royal Forest', a hunting reserve of the Neapolitan kings). Until a few years ago the name was known principally to art historians, from the discovery there in 1895 of the Boscoreale Treasure, in a cistern of the Villa della Pisanella. Hastily hidden at the beginning of the eruption in AD 79, 1000 gold coins, jewellery and 109 pieces of silverware were found next to a man's skeleton. The Villa della Pisanella, which no longer survives, became the type-site for study of the *villae rusticae*, with its living quarters, slave

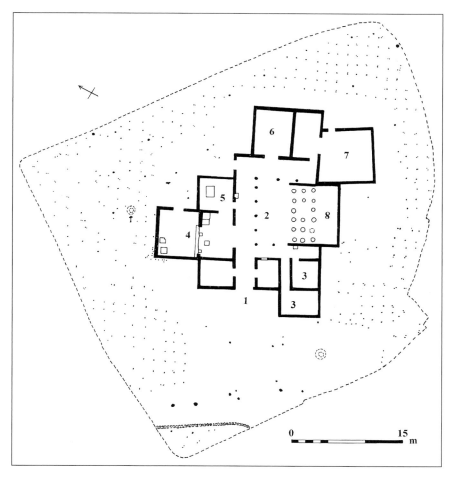

51 Boscoreale, *villa rustica* at Villa Regina: 1. Entrance; 2. Peristyle; 3. Living area; 4. Wine-making area; 5. Kitchen; 6. *Triclinium*; 7. Threshing floor; 8. Yard with *dolia* set in floor. (After De Caro 1994)

accommodation, bath suite and a courtyard set with *dolia* (large terracotta jars) for storing wine.

However, there is a new attraction (*colour plate 12*). Tucked away amid a modern housing estate called Villa Regina is a *villa rustica* found during development in 1977, and since fully reconstructed. To reach it from the site entrance of Pompeii walk north on Via Villa dei Misteri, then make a left and a right turn, under then over the railway line on Via Andolfi, right on to Via Settetermini, and soon left again on to Via Promiscua till the perimeter wall of the site comes into view, about 25 minutes in all. Care is need if approaching on foot from Pompeii. Alternatively, the site can be reached from the rail station of Boscoreale on the Circumvesuviana line heading for Poggiomarino, then by following Via Settetermini on foot or by bus. By car use the exit 'Pompei' from Autostrada A3. There is parking at the site within its walled precinct. (Hours: April – October 8.30–19.30; November – March 8.30–17.00. Closed 1 January, 1 May and 25 December.)

Excavated and published in exemplary fashion, the villa had been buried by Vesuvius in AD 79 to a depth of up to 5.9m, and by a further 2m in later eruptions. Initially laid out in the aftermath of the Sullan colonisation at Pompeii, possibly for a newly arrived army veteran, but extended in the Augustan period to something approaching its final layout, this was not a luxury establishment but a modest farm, worked by a single family and their slaves, devoted principally to producing wine (*51*). The latter was stored on site in 18 terracotta *dolia*, buried to their necks, some found with their lids still in place (*52*). The roof-tiles above the portico, which were stamped with the names of local manufacturers, were found more or less in situ at their original height off the ground, where pumice and ashy material had effectively oozed into and filled the spaces below. Finds included the iron fitments of a two-wheeled wooden cart. The environs of the farmhouse were laid out with neat lines of vines, some 300 in all, supported on poles, together with olive trees and some fruit trees including peach, fig and apricot. The age of the vines could indicate a recent programme of replanting. Overall we see here the agricultural economy of the farmstead and almost feel that we can look out, as the owner must have done, on the cultivated ground stretching away from his house.

The adjacent museum houses two interconnected displays. The first, devoted to the economy and environment of the region in Roman times, is enhanced by a copy of the famous plaster cast of a dog from Pompeii, and another of a domestic pig found in one of the villa's rooms during

52 Boscoreale, wine-storage jars (*dolia*) at the *villa rustica*. (L. Keppie)

the excavations. The second section details the many villas excavated in the neighbourhood, including the Villa della Pisanella where the 'Boscoreale Treasure' (above, p. 119) was found in 1895, and another at one time owned by P. Fannius Synistor, from which many fine wall-paintings datable to 50–40 BC, in the Second Style, are now displayed in a specially built room at the Metropolitan Museum of Art, New York. A property found in 1903 at nearby Boscotrecase is tentatively linked to Augustus' lieutenant Agrippa who died hereabouts in 12 BC. Many of its elegant black and yellow wall-paintings are similarly housed in New York and others in Naples.

13. Pompeii

Pompeii must rank among the busiest archaeological sites in the world. The modern visitor will not be alone, and in high season the streets are at least as crowded as they must have been in ancient times. Access to the site is principally from the train station Pompei Scavi, Villa dei Misteri, on the Circumvesuviana railway, after a short walk past souvenir stalls to the Marine Gate entrance. By car, exit from the A3 Autostrada at Pompei ovest or at

Pompei est if northbound. (Hours: April – October 8.30–19.30; November – March 8.30–17.00. Closed 1 January, 1 May and 25 December.) The Pompei Santuario train station on the Circumvesuviana line to Poggiomarino, and the FS/Trenitalia station at Pompei are both in the modern town, some distance east of the archaeological site. Notices at the entrance tell the watchful which buildings or houses are currently closed for restoration work, or are open only to visitors who book in advance on the internet (www.arethusa.net) or at the ticket windows. There are toilets here and a mercifully air-conditioned bookshop. Access can also be achieved to the far end of the site from an entrance in Piazza Anfiteatro in the modern town.

The itinerary outlined below assumes that a whole day is available, but even so it is important to call a halt before exhaustion sets in. In general it is good to plan a route before arriving at the site, or when pausing at the Forum. Many will find themselves at the distant amphitheatre at the hottest time of the day, and the lengthy upwards trek towards the main site entrance and the railway station still awaits them. One means of avoiding this return journey is to exit the site at the amphitheatre, and walk back to the train station round the southern flank of the site. All this said, of course, Pompeii is a wonderfully exhilarating experience. Ideally the visitor should aim to reach the site by 9am when there is still hope of long vistas of nearly empty streets, the sun is low and crowds still to arrive, with Vesuvius just behind and the prominent Monti Lattari rising up southwards. As many tour groups make just a morning visit, the independent traveller will find the site quieter after lunchtime, though at its hottest. Once inside, the visitor should take the time to pinpoint the café-restaurant immediately north of the Forum, i.e. behind the *Capitolium*, which is the only place inside the site where one can currently purchase bottled water, have lunch and use the toilet facilities. Numerous standpipes for drinking water have recently been installed.

It is difficult, as at Herculaneum, to appreciate the original topographical situation of the town, which was on a plateau overlooking the mouth of the River Sarno where the latter debouched into the Bay (53). A quay close to the Marine Gate is equipped with perforated mooring stones. Houses on the town's south-west flank were terraced over the seafront. Nowadays the site lies 1.7km inland, and the Sarno follows a quite different course to the sea.

A relatively recent innovation has been the creation of a wall-walk round the town's defensive perimeter, allowing a perambulation of over half of the walls. One can, for example, start from the Herculaneum Gate and proceed in a clockwise direction past views of walling, gates, modern working farms

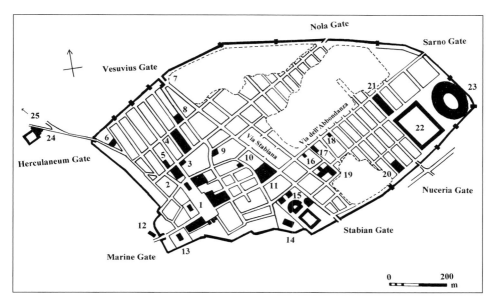

53 Pompeii, buildings referred to in the text: 1. Forum; 2. Forum Baths; 3. Temple of *Fortuna Augusta*; 4. House of the Faun; 5. House of the Tragic Poet; 6. House of the Surgeon; 7. Water-distribution tank; 8. House of the Vettii; 9. Bakery of Popidius Priscus; 10. Brothel; 11. Stabian Baths; 12. Suburban Baths; 13. Temple of Venus; 14. Triangular Forum; 15. Theatres; 16. Laundry of Stephanus; 17. House of Paquius Proculus; 18. Bar of Vetutius Placidus; 19. House of the Menander; 20. Garden of the Fugitives; 21. House of Octavius Quartio; 22. Palaestra; 23. Amphitheatre; 24. Villa of Diomedes; 25. Villa of the Mysteries

and allotments beyond the excavated areas, on a specially laid pathway past an attractive picnic area with wooden benches, to the Nola Gate, which is currently inaccessible from the main site. There the path descends to a little piazza lined with tombs, with seating for the weary traveller. Then, skirting the main Naples–Salerno railway line, the visitor reaches the amphitheatre and can continue onwards to the Nuceria Gate.

It used to be thought that the original nucleus of the Roman town was on the headland now occupied by the Triangular Forum and the adjacent theatre complex (below, p. 132). However, more recent excavation has suggested that a wider area was occupied from a quite early date, all of it enclosed before the end of the sixth century BC by walls, though some of the interior long remained unused. The walls were pierced at intervals by gates, from which roads led away into the countryside, heading for adjacent towns, and later equipped with interval towers. In the immediate aftermath of the Social War of 90–89 BC Pompeii received a Roman colony, established by the victor, Cornelius Sulla, but only after a siege reflected in the archaeological record, which includes indentations in the walls left by lead slingbullets and large stone ballista balls, examples of which have been recovered in the course of excavation. Army veterans were implanted on its territory, and the town received a new name, *colonia Veneria Cornelia Pompeianorum*, *Veneria* commemorating Venus, the patron goddess of Sulla himself, and *Cornelia* deriving from his family name, Cornelius; at this time the town acquired a prominently situated temple of Venus, overlooking the sea. Pompeii's buildings, both public and private, suffered serious damage in the earthquake of AD 62–3 (above, p. 22), and possibly in other earthquakes in the years that followed.

There is no space here to discuss every surviving building in detail; the reader is referred to the numerous published handbooks (see Bibliography at p. 184). Signs are in Italian and English; there are audio-tours, and on-site guides can still be hired. The colourful site-plan given out at the entrance, though at a separate window from the tickets, highlights buildings most worth a visit. After negotiating any queues at the ticket offices and the automated turnstiles, the visitor ascends the paved roadway to the arched Marine Gate, passing on the left the recently restored Suburban Baths, well worth a visit if open (To book a visit, go to www.arethusa.net). The main rooms, in a conventional sequence, have much of their heating systems intact (54). In AD 79 some parts were undergoing repairs. Painted scenes high up on walls in the *apodyterium* graphically illustrate individually numbered erotic scenes, which some consider were delectations available to male clients in rooms on an upper storey now lost, including three-on-a-couch options. The visitor, following the sloping ramp up to the Marine Gate, gains an immediate impression of being transported back in time, with a first sight of the neatly laid volcanic paving.

It is a short onwards walk to the Forum, where the visitor needs to make a crucial decision, either to walk the length of the Via dell'Abbondanza towards the amphitheatre, which should be undertaken as early in the day as possible, returning perhaps via the theatres and the Temple of Isis towards the Forum (the sequence adopted in the following pages), or alternatively to undertake a more modest itinerary, taking in some houses, the theatres and the ever popular brothel, before retiring to the cool of the café for restorative food and drink. After lunch, the visitor with more time can proceed northwards, past the Forum Baths in the general direction of

54 Pompeii, Suburban Baths outside the Marine Gate

the Herculaneum Gate, then down the Street of the Tombs to the Villa of the Mysteries. There is probably no ideal route, and each visitor needs to decide what suits his fancy, his family's interests and his stamina. Of course wandering at will has its frequent rewards. Some streets are permanently closed off because of remedial works in progress, so that detours may be needed to reach a chosen destination.

The visitor walking into Pompeii from the Marine Gate soon arrives at the south end of the Forum, which did not lie centrally, but nearer the western end of the town, perhaps indicative of stages in its expansion. Statues in stone and bronze were set on the surviving solid plinths at its edges. On the right was the town's colonnaded lawcourt (*basilica*), perhaps roofed over, and close by lay the modestly proportioned meeting places for the *Ordo Decurionum* and for the pairs of annually elected magistrates. Nearly was a square hall, interpreted as the *comitium*, where votes were cast in municipal elections.

The once paved Forum, now cordoned off and grassed over to reduce dust-storms on windy days, was enclosed by a two-storey portico of which some elements have been re-erected (*colour plate 13*). At the far (northern) end, flanked by ornamental archways, was the *Capitolium*, a temple dedicated to Jupiter, Juno and Minerva jointly, the symbol of the town's colonial status.

Opening off the long sides of the Forum were public buildings (55) including, on its right side, the *macellum* (the shape recalling the *Serapeum* at Puteoli) where plaster casts of two bodies are displayed in cases, and the Building of Eumachia, a large colonnaded court of uncertain purpose, but proposed as the guildhouse of the laundrymen who erected a statue to

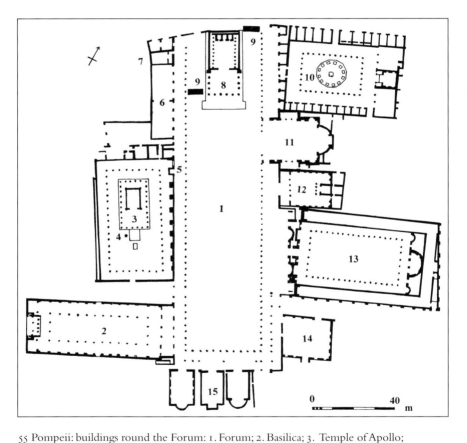

55 Pompeii: buildings round the Forum: 1. Forum; 2. Basilica; 3. Temple of Apollo;
4. Sundial; 5. Weights and measures table; 6. Vegetable market; 7. Latrine; 8. *Capitolium*;
9 Arch; 10. *Macellum*; 11. Sanctuary of the town's Guardian Spirits; 12. 'Temple of Vespasian';
13. Building of Eumachia; 14. Hall for holding elections; 15. Offices. (After Ward-Perkins and Claridge 1976)

her. Temples included one to the *Genius* (Spirit) of Augustus, sometimes (wrongly it seems) called the 'Temple of Vespasian'; the large marble altar in front depicts a ceremony of purification, at which a bull was sacrificed to ensure the emperor's well-being (5). Next to it is a large open courtyard, the Sanctuary of the *Lares Publici*, the town's guardian spirits.

A rectangular precinct on the left of the Forum housed the Temple of Apollo on a raised podium (*colour plate 14*). The central cell was enclosed by columns on all four sides in the Greek manner, rather than only at the front. The altar lay at the foot of stone steps. A replica bronze statue of Apollo, the original found elsewhere in the town, is erected here as its likely original placing. Next to the steps is a column topped by a sundial, the rectangular inscribed panel identifying the donors as L. Sepunius and M. Herennius, *Duoviri* under Augustus. A 'weights and measures' table was sited in an alcove of its precinct wall, facing the Forum. The accuracy of the measures is testified to by the names of the responsible *Duoviri*.

On the left side of the Forum towards its northern end is an area of 'displayed storage' in the vegetable market, where some of the most familiar, if rather dust-covered, exhibits from a former site-museum, including plaster casts of a hunched-up youth (*11*) and of the famous chained-up dog, are on view behind grilles. At the far north-west corner of the Forum was a multi-seater latrine, still under construction at the time of the eruption, its interior shielded from public view by the carefully sited door.

After exploring the Forum, the visitor is likely to proceed eastwards along the broad Via dell'Abbondanza, leading eventually to the palaestra and amphitheatre (below, p. 131). Some distance along the street is the town's principal crossroads, sometimes called the Holconius Crossroads, where the Via dell'Abbondanza intersected with the Via Stabiana, the town's chief north-south artery (*4*). A barrier prevented wheeled traffic from ascending towards the Forum. Brick supports mark the position of a four-wayed arch spanning the Via dell'Abbondanza, in front of which stood statues of M. Holconius Rufus and members of his family, prominent under Augustus. Nowadays visitors throng to slake their thirst at the welcome stone fountain at one corner, next to a lofty brick-built water-pressure tower which once served it. Large stepping stones, still much in use, facilitated crossing.

The advantageously placed Stabian Baths, constructed in the second century BC, lay nearby on the north side of the Via dell'Abbondanza. Access was gained from the street to a grand peristyle courtyard, on the left of which was a large rectangular swimming pool with elaborate wall-paintings, and on the right the conventional sequence of heated rooms with fine stuccoed ceilings, whose heating systems can be detected below the floors and in the walls. Separate facilities for women lay behind, accessed from the flanking side-streets. In the *apodyterium* are two antique display cases, each containing the plaster cast of a Pompeian in his death agonies.

A little to the north-east of the Forum, at the junction between the Vicolo Storto and the Vicolo del Panettiere, the visitor will find the Bakery of N. Popidius Priscus, one of many such establishments in the town. Stone grinding equipment was turned by mules; the brick-built oven would not look out of place in a good pizzeria (*colour plate 15*). A brothel (*lupanar*), one of several in Pompeii, lies some distance north of the Stabian Baths in the Vico di Lupanare. Five rooms of varying size opened off a central hall, the plastered walls displaying graffiti left by the prostitutes and their clients. Above eye level are painted scenes depicting sexual positions. More rooms, perhaps for a higher-class clientele, were on an upper floor, reached by a separate stairway from the street.

A large number of election notices (see above, p. 31), painted on exterior house-walls along the Via dell'Abbondanza, especially on its north side east of the crossroads, advertise in red the names of candidates and their supporters. They are protected nowadays, after a fashion, by sheets of perspex and miniature awnings. Notices jostling for position on the walls exhorted the reader to elect, for example, C. Popidius as *aedile*, others C. Lollius Fuscus for the same post, probably (but not certainly) in the elections held in spring AD 79 (*colour plate 16*). Others asked the viewer to support Ceius Secundus for the post of chief magistrate, *duovir iure dicundo*.

On the south side of the Via dell'Abbondanza, east of the Holconius Crossroads, lies the Laundry of Stephanus, converted from a private residence and equipped with a series of tanks for washing clothes in a mixture of water and urine, and facilities for drying clothes on the roof. The floor of the nearby entrance to the House of Paquius Proculus (beyond the alley named after him) has a dog sitting full-length in black-and-white mosaic, with a representation of the house's half-open double doors behind it, to one of which the dog is attached by a chain.

Of the many bars and food outlets in the town, one of the most evocative is the Bar of Vetutius Placidus, further along the street. The colourful *lararium* at the far end of its counter shows Mercury, god of trade, and Bacchus, god of wine, with protective serpents below (*colour plate 17*). *Dolia* to contain foodstuffs were incorporated in the counter. One *dolium* was found on excavation to contain a very large amount of small change, perhaps accumulated takings. Vetutius' house lay immediately behind the shop.

Further along the Via dell'Abbondanza is the House of 'Loreius Tiburtinus' (more likely to have belonged to D. Octavius Quartio), with its finely painted rooms and its replanted garden of fruit trees (*56*). Passing through a double door represented in plaster casts, the visitor arrives at the *atrium*, beyond which was a small enclosed garden, with a square mosaic-floored *triclinium* to one side. Immediately behind the house itself was an east-west water channel, at right angles to the axis of the house, with a two-couch dining room at one end for summertime use.

The main *triclinium* was carefully positioned to look out directly on to the long axis of the garden, which stretched the full width of the block. A water-filled channel extended its entire length, topped by fountains (*colour plate 18*). The wooden trellis has been re-erected on the basis of stakeholes found during excavation. The channel used to be enlivened by working fountains and flowing water. This house appears to have originally occupied the entire block, but its north-east quarter was later separated to form another dwelling.

One block further east, on the same side of the street, is the House of Venus in a Shell, with its peaceful garden and eponymous wall-painting showing Venus, newly risen from the waves, being transported to land by

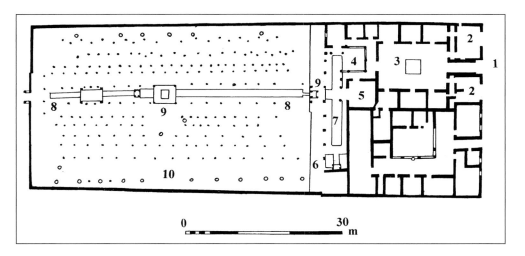

56 Pompeii, House of 'Loreius Tiburtinus': 1. Entrance; 2. Shop; 3. *Atrium*; 4. Small garden; 5. *Triclinium*; 6. Summer dining room; 7. East-west water channel; 8. North-south water channel; 9. Fountain; 10. Garden. (After La Rocca, De Vos and De Vos 1976)

cupids riding on dolphins. Turning southwards off the Via dell'Abbondanza a few blocks further to the east into the Vicolo dei Fuggiaschi, the visitor will find, towards its lower end on the right, a garden in which plaster casts of 13 victims of the eruption are placed on view under protective covers, one man struggling to get up as the ash closed over him.

One block short of the palaestra, downhill on the Via di Nocera, visitors step unconcernedly over the concrete water-channel whose laying down in 1594–1600 led to the initial discovery of the site, an event commemorated on an adjacent wall-mounted plaque. The Via di Nocera leads down to the Nuceria Gate, beyond which one can look back to admire the walls of the town stretching away to either side. The relative absence of the usual throngs allows a contemplative visit. At the crossroads beyond the gate, a square pillar commemorates the work of L. Suedius Clemens during Vespasian's reign in recovering for the town ground encroached on by developers, perhaps in the aftermath of the AD 62–63 earthquake.

Tombs in a variety of styles extended parallel to the walls and very probably also southwards under the modern town of Pompei. Many are 'house-tombs' containing the burials of entire families (*colour plate 19*).

57 Pompeii, view across the Palaestra

Stucco facings have fallen away to reveal the brick and stone structures. The lofty tomb of M. Octavius and his freedwoman wife, Vertia Philumina (on the opposite side of the road, west of the gate), takes the form of a temple on a high podium (*10*); between the columns stand tuff statues of Octavius in military uniform, flanked by a man and a woman, probably his parents. At its base are niches for memorials to the family's slaves. The nearby square tomb of the Tillius family is defaced by a painted notice advertising '20 pairs of gladiators' in forthcoming games at the amphitheatre of nearby Nuceria. Both tombs are likely to date to the first century BC and may commemorate men who fought in the civil wars of the Late Republic. Pumice layers are in places visible in section.

Just inside the walls, at the south-east corner of the town, were two major public amenities, the palaestra and the amphitheatre. The palaestra, constructed in the reign of Augustus, was a large open exercise area and sports ground bounded on all four sides by porticoes, with a swimming pool at its centre (*57*). Lines of trees, identified from their roots, provided shade.

The amphitheatre is among the earliest such structures known, predating the Colosseum in Rome by about 150 years. It was built in the decade following Pompeii's elevation to the status of a Roman colony in 80 BC by the *Duoviri* C. Quinctius Valgus and M. Porcius, as inscriptions, one (a cast) now wall-mounted in the southern access tunnel, proclaim. The inscription (*58*), whose left side is broken away, does not actually use the word *amphitheatrum*, but states that Valgus and Porcius gave *spectacula*, 'shows', or perhaps 'places of entertainment', which they presented to their fellow colonists in perpetuity. Two other inscriptions, set rather unobtrusively into the walls of the north access-tunnel, record unspecified work by a father and son, both named C. Cuspius Pansa, magistrates in the town during Nero's reign; they probably oversaw repairs to the amphitheatre after the earthquake in AD 62-3.

The arena was scooped out and the spoil used to create an oval embankment topped by a skin of stone seating, which accommodated up to 20,000 spectators, divided by horizontal stone barriers according to class and status (*colour plate 20*). Distinctive external gangways allowed direct access to the upper tiers across a walkway (*59*), and shade was originally provided by awnings. The amphitheatre hosted gladiatorial fights and wild beast hunts. In AD 59, when tempers boiled over among the audience, as Tacitus reports, fighting broke out between the locals and visitors from Nuceria across the plain to the east. As a result the games' sponsors were

58 Pompeii, inscription commemorating the construction of the amphitheatre *c*.80 BC

exiled, unspecified 'clubs' were banned and the amphitheatre itself closed for 10 years. The whole event is memorably depicted on a wall-painting now in Naples (above, p. 85), which vividly shows swordfights both inside the arena and in the open space outside next to the palaestra. As two sides of the amphitheatre were set against the town wall, access to the arena and to the lower tiers of seating could be had only from the west and north. Once inside it is easy to forget that this is not a completely freestanding structure.

The visitor can now return westwards on the Via di Castricio, flanking the north side of the palaestra, to a T-junction beyond which lies the sprawling House of the Menander, named for a painting of this Greek poet in one of the rooms which were elegantly decorated with fine mosaics and wall-paintings (access at weekends, when booked in advance on www.arethusa.net). A small underground cellar yielded a remarkable cache of silverware stored in a wooden box.

Continuing westwards along the Vicolo del Menandro, one of the town's most attractive districts is reached, centred round the theatre and the Triangular Forum, an angular porticoed enclosure, nowadays shaded and welcoming (*60*). The Triangular Forum housed a Greek-style Doric temple of great antiquity dedicated to Minerva or to Hercules, or both, which some

59 Pompeii, external gangways of the amphitheatre

think was disused by the time the volcano erupted. Close by was a circular columned structure (a *tholos*), housing a well-head.

Immediately behind the theatre, and likely to be visited before it, are two buildings along the Via del Tempio d'Iside. First is the Samnite Palaestra, a colonnaded courtyard laid out in the second century BC (as an inscription testifies), and interpreted as a small exercise area. Next to it is a splendid temple to the Egyptian goddess Isis (*61*). A modest gateway, above which is a copy of an inscribed tablet commemorating the six-year-old Popidius Celsinus who nominally financed its complete rebuilding after the earthquake of AD 62–3, gives access to the precinct. Inside are the plaster-covered brick walls and columns of the temple façade, with an altar placed to one side at the foot of the access steps. When the altar was excavated in 1765 (*colour plate 2*), ashes and burnt bone were found atop it, suggested as debris from a recent sacrifice. In front of the temple, on the left, was a roofless compartment with a pool for sacred Nile water, used in the purification of worshippers, reached by descending some steps. A rectangular hall behind the temple, once decorated with scenes from the Isis cult, perhaps served for banquets. An attractive model of the temple is on view at the Archaeological Museum in Naples.

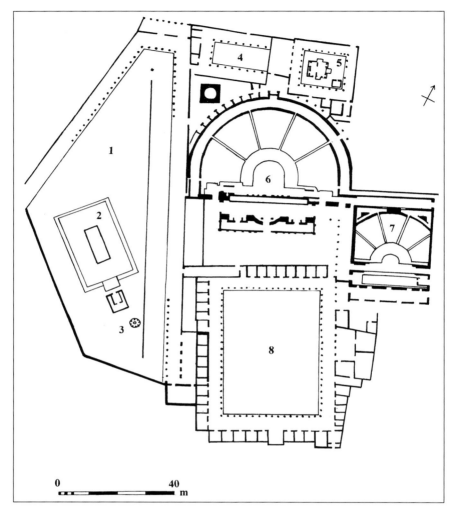

60 Pompeii, Triangular Forum and Theatre Precinct: 1. Triangular Forum; 2. Doric Temple; 3. Columned well-head; 4. Samnite Palaestra; 5. Temple of Isis; 6. Theatre; 7. Covered theatre; 8. Portico. (After La Rocca, De Vos and De Vos 1976)

The theatre, with a capacity of some 5000, was set against the natural southwards slope of the ground (*colour plate 21*). Cassius Dio, in his romanticised account of the eruption written well over a century after the event, has the populace sitting in the theatre when the eruption began. Originally constructed in the second century BC, the theatre was rebuilt

61   Pompeii, Temple of Isis

in the Augustan period at the expense of the Holconius family, whose beneficence is commemorated in several inscriptions. The stage itself was backed by a substantial two-storey façade, now largely robbed out; the ancient audience thus had a more restricted view than the modern visitor. The seating and stage have on occasion been re-covered in timber to allow concerts to be held. An invasion by a pack of dogs in the summer of 2007 interrupted a performance.

Rather later in date was a smaller, covered theatre (*odeum*) seating some 1000 spectators, which nestled against its bigger neighbour, and was erected in about 80 BC under the supervision of the same pair of magistrates who oversaw the construction of the amphitheatre (above, p. 131); it served for musical recitals, mimes and recitations. The seating terminated at both ends in kneeling Atlas-like figures called *telamones*, supporting small plinths which were perhaps once topped by statuettes. The covered theatre may, it is suggested, have also hosted meetings of the Town Council, the *Ordo Decurionum*.

On lower ground in front of the larger theatre was a large, four-sided portico (*quadriporticus*), probably serving initially as space for spectators to congregate or promenade between performances; to one side was a large banqueting hall. After the earthquake in AD 62–3, part served to accommodate gladiators, some of whose elaborate equipment, including helmets, was found there.

Next, preferably after a rest, a toilet break at the cafeteria near the Forum, and coffee or a cold drink, the modern visitor may make immediately for the adjacent Forum Baths, northwards in the same block (*62*). Its public face onto the streets was largely taken up by shops, between which several narrow entrances gave access to the baths and to an exercise courtyard. After recent renovation, visitors are required to follow a set route on protective carpeting, which makes the whole experience less satisfying than hitherto, and hinders photography.

The Forum Baths are complete to ceiling level, which helps to emphasise their compactness. Light was admitted through glazed windows. The *apodyterium* was lined with masonry benches, nail holes above suggesting wooden shelving; off it opened a circular cold bath. Next the bather passed through a wooden door into the *tepidarium*, with magnificent stucco decoration; niches against the walls were for towels and unguents. This room had no inbuilt heating system, but was warmed by a brazier on view behind a railing at the end of the room. The brazier bears the name of its donor, M. Nigidius Vaccula. Here, and on the flanking bronze benches, cow-motifs jocularly recall the donor's surname, which means 'heifer'. The niches above were attractively demarcated by standing male *telamones* ('supporters'). Another doorway led to the *caldarium*, where we can see the cavity system behind the plastered walls, up which the heat travelled to the ceiling; moisture flowed back down to the floor in parallel channels in the stucco. At one end was an oblong hot bath, and at the other a circular marble basin (*63*), whose lip bears in bronze lettering the names of Cn. Melissaeus Aper and M. Staius Rufus, *Duoviri* in AD 3–4, and the cost in sesterces to the public purse. The women's section, tucked into the north-west corner

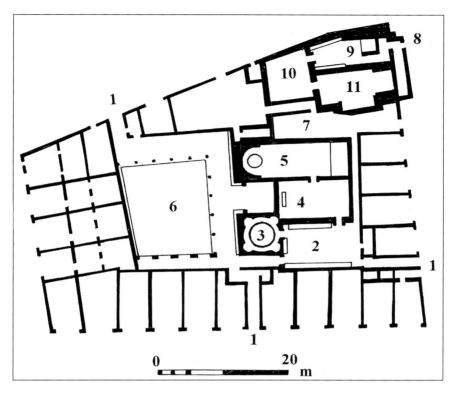

62 Pompeii, the Forum Baths: Men's suite, 1. Entrances; 2. *Apodyterium*; 3. Circular cold bath; 4. *Tepidarium*; 5. *Caldarium*; 6. Peristyle; 7. *Praefurnium*. Women's suite, 8. Entrance; 9. *Apodyterium* with Cold Bath; 10. *Tepidarium*; 11. *Caldarium*. (After La Rocca, De Vos and De Vos 1976)

of the block, was a much more modest establishment. A porticoed exercise yard, southwards off the main range of heated rooms, has long formed part of the adjacent restaurant.

Next, one option is to head eastwards along the Via della Fortuna, past the Temple of *Fortuna Augusta* (the emperor's Good Fortune), built at the expense of M. Tullius on his own land-plot in honour of Augustus. The House of the Faun, opening northwards off the same street, is named for a bronze statuette, a copy of which stands in the centre of the *impluvium*. The house, whose owners in AD 79 are unknown, was initially laid out in the early second century BC, and enlarged some decades later, perhaps by building over the extensive garden. In its final form the house occupied an entire *insula*. Beyond its *atrium* and the reception room was a peristyle

63 Pompeii, circular basin in the *caldarium* of the Forum Baths

garden in the normal fashion, but beyond that were other rooms, and a second, even larger peristyle. In a large room fronted by columns, between the two peristyles, was found the famous floor mosaic now at Naples depicting Alexander victorious over the Persian King Darius (above, p. 85); a pale copy has recently been placed in the original position.

The visitor can now turn northwards, using either the Vicolo dei Vetti or the Vicolo del Labirinto, to arrive at the House of the Vettii (currently closed for restoration), one block behind the House of the Faun. The House of the Vettii (64), often cited as the 'typical' Pompeian family home, was bought after the AD 62–3 earthquake and lavishly redecorated according to the latest fashions by two freedman brothers, Vettius Conviva and Vettius Restitutus, who seem likely to have made their money as wine merchants. Near the entrance the painted image of Priapus, god of fertility and protector of the house and its garden, weighing his phallus against a heavy bag of coins, served as a good luck image. Formerly kept out of sight inside a locked wooden cupboard, it adds to the house's continuing popularity. Conspicuously placed in the *atrium* on masonry plinths to either side of the *impluvium* were wooden strongboxes, strengthened with iron bars and decorated with bronze fitments, which advertised the owners' wealth.

The visitor's eye will be immediately caught by the large peristyle garden which lies beyond, tastefully furnished with marble tables and cupid fountains in bronze and marble. To one side of the *atrium* was the service wing with its kitchen and a delightful *lararium* set against the wall (*8*). Stairs led to an upper storey. Expensive wall-paintings throughout the house, painted after the earthquake of AD 62–3, depict mythological scenes. Cupids harvesting grapes, the subject matter likely to reflect the business interests of the new owners, decorated the walls of a room, the likely *triclinium*, facing onto the peristyle. A one-way system operates for modern visitors to the

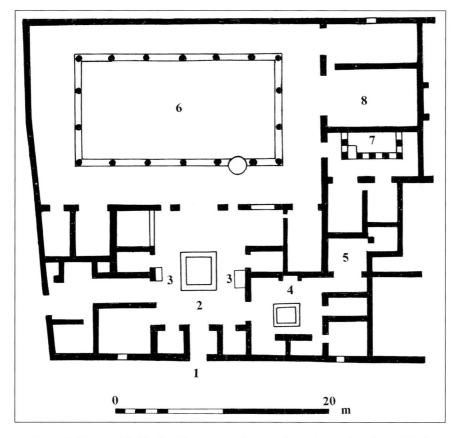

64 Pompeii, House of the Vettii: 1. Entrance; 2. *Atrium*; 3. Strongbox; 4. *Lararium*; 5. Kitchen; 6. Peristyle; 7. Enclosed garden; 8. *Triclinium*. (After La Rocca, De Vos and De Vos 1976)

65 Pompeii, water-distribution tank (*castellum aquae*) inside the Vesuvius Gate

house, who enter through the front door in the Vicolo dei Vetti and exit into the Vicolo di Mercurio. Notice the lead water-piping exposed at pavement level outside.

Northwards, rather off the main tourist track, the visitor can proceed to the end of the Vicolo dei Vetti, or the parallel Via del Vesuvio, a northwards continuation of the Via Stabiana, to the *castellum aquae* (65) just inside the Vesuvius Gate, beyond which a few tombs are exposed. The Victorian-looking brick-built *castellum*, familiar from Robert Harris' *Pompeii,* was a water-distribution tank which received the flow from the Aqua Augusta. (Here the visitor can, if desired, use the walkway on the alignment of the town walls to go directly westwards to the Herculaneum Gate, and visit the attractions listed below in a reverse order.)

Alternatively, and starting again from the Forum, the visitor may strike north-westwards, taking in the narrow entrance to the House of the Tragic Poet (on Via delle Terme, directly behind the Forum Baths), on the floor of which is the famous *cave canem* mosaic (7). In Bulwer-Lytton's *Last Days of Pompeii* (1834), the home of the novel's leading character Glaucus was based on this house, excavated in 1824–25.

Further along the Via Consolare, on the right after the road splits, are the House of the Surgeon and the House of the Vestals, both explored for many years in an international project by an Anglo–American team led by the University of Bradford (*colour plate 24*).

The massive Herculaneum Gate marked the north-west corner of the town, where the walls turned at a sharp angle. Beyond the Gate itself the road drops away, flanked by splendid, recently cleaned tombs, several in the form of funerary altars, their dedicatory inscriptions reporting the names and achievements of the deceased (*66*). Semicircular seating, as useful to the weary modern visitor as to the ancient traveller waiting outside in the morning for the gate to be opened, marked out the tomb of Mamia, member of a prominent local family, with the letters of her name carved in sequence along the stone backrests. Some monuments commemorated long-resident wealthy families, others newly rich freedmen. Some were for individuals, others for whole families, together with their slaves, in clearly defined enclosures.

The small arched Tomb of M. Cerrinius Restitutus immediately outside the Herculaneum Gate (on the left, as the visitor descends) resembles a rural bus shelter. It was once interpreted from its position as a sentry box, and the story of a soldier's skeleton having been found inside it soon developed, to be immortalised in Bulwer-Lytton's *Last Days of Pompeii* (1834) and in the painting by Sir Edward Poynter entitled *Faithful unto Death* (1865). Interspersed with the tombs are rows of shops. Many of the tombs were built on plots presented to the families by the Town Council.

A fine slab, set on the front of one of the tombs on the left (but belonging, it may be, to the next tomb downhill), commemorates A. Umbricius Scaurus, of a Pompeian family producing the distinctive *garum* fish-sauce; the inscription reports that the *Ordo Decurionum* had voted 2000 sesterces for his funeral, and ordained that a statue to him on horseback was to be erected in the Forum. One of the most memorable of the prominent altar-shaped tombs is that of C. Calventius Quietus (on the left, walking downhill), an *Augustalis*, with his honorary magistrate's chair (as a freedman he was ineligible to hold office) and civic crowns on the altar's sides. Further down the slope stands the tomb of Naevoleia Tyche and her husband C. Munatius Faustus, another *Augustalis*; on one side a sailing ship, carved in relief, is entering harbour, a scene thought to symbolise not trade, but the soul's voyage to the underworld (*67*). On the other side of the street, higher up the slope, is the arched 'Tomb of the Villa of Mosaic Columns', richly

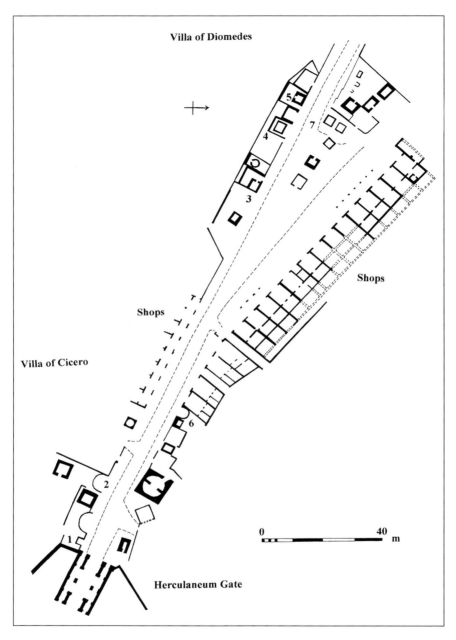

66 Pompeii, tombs outside the Herculaneum Gate: 1. M. Cerrinius Restitutus; 2. The priestess Mamia; 3. A. Umbricius Scaurus; 4. C. Calventius Quietus; 5. Naevoleia Tyche and C. Munatius Faustus; 6. Tomb of the Villa of the Mosaic Columns; 7. M. Alleius Luccius Libella. (After Kockel 1983)

decorated with white stucco, with an unused panel for an inscription set in the pediment above, and seating below the arch. Where the road splits, monuments vie for position, including the well-proportioned altar-tomb erected to the magistrate M. Alleius Luccius Libella by his wife.

On the left, two extramural villas enjoyed the fine but now much restricted views. One, long ago named for Cicero, was reached from a modest entrance not far beyond the Herculaneum Gate, but only its outline plan is known. A little further downhill, the Villa of Diomedes, named for a freedman whose tomb lies nearby, is similarly set at an angle to the street. This villa has all the standard features, here on two levels, the lower opening onto a large porticoed garden overlooking the sea, with pools and fountains. Some 20 skeletons were found when it was excavated in the eighteenth century.

Beyond the foot of the slope, past an old entry-gate to the site, is the extramural Villa of the Mysteries, set on a concrete platform which served to even up a sloping site (*68*). Begun in the second century BC, the villa was much enlarged in the early first century BC and subsequently, until it boasted some 60 rooms. The visitor arrives first at the sea-facing apartments, where a semicircular apse overlooked the Bay, flanked by porticoes. However, the formal entrance was from a road running past the villa on the north-east

67 Pompeii, tombs outside the Herculaneum Gate, including those of C. Calventius Quietus (centre) and of C. Munatius Faustus and Naevoleia Tyche (right)

side, through a vestibule and a peristyle with, unusually, the *atrium* beyond it. A bath suite lay on one side of the peristyle and a smaller apsed room on the other. Particularly memorable are the wall-paintings in the Second Style, dated to the mid-first century BC, in its south-west quarter, showing the painful initiation of a young woman into the mysteries of Dionysus. The room itself is interpreted as a *triclinium*. In the final years of its existence several of the rooms were converted to agricultural purposes, probably to process the produce from adjacent farmland. One room now houses the handsome replica of a wine-press, with a wooden ram's-head pole.

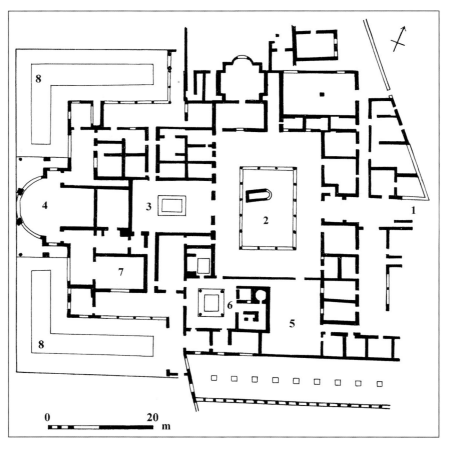

68 Pompeii, Villa of the Mysteries: 1. Entrance from Roman street; 2. Peristyle; **3.** *Atrium*; 4. Apsidal room facing the Bay; 5. Kitchen; 6. Baths; 7. Hall of the Mysteries; 8. Garden. (After La Rocca, De Vos and De Vos 1976)

The visitor can exit the site here, or will more likely return by climbing the slope between the lines of tombs – it always seems steeper on the return journey – to the Herculaneum Gate, and in due course to the Forum. Visitors are currently directed to leave the site by skirting the large Temple of Venus, recently under investigation by a sizeable international team led by the University of Basilicata. Nero and his wife Poppaea gave expensive gifts to the temple on a visit to Pompeii in AD 63–5. (Pass through a barrier and then rightwards along a tree-lined avenue to arrive again at the main entrance and the train station.)

The visitor can also leave the site at the amphitheatre into the modern town of Pompei, which grew rapidly in the later nineteenth century round the Santuario della Madonna del Rosario in Piazza Bartolo Longo. The sanctuary receives as many visitors a year as the archaeological site, consequently attracting a McDonald's restaurant. The Museo Vesuviano 'G. B. Alfano' (Via Colle S. Bartolomeo, 10) has samples of material expelled by the volcano and many framed engravings of its eruptions through the ages. (Hours: 8.30–14.00, Monday – Friday.)

South of Pompeii, Roman buildings have been detected on a ridge of high ground along the shore and beside the River Sarno. In 56–5 BC Cicero congratulated his friend M. Marius for knocking a window through a wall in his country villa near Pompeii, which gave him an enchanting view of the coastline southwards towards Stabiae. At Moregine, a name also now given to a new station on the Circumvesuviana railway heading for Castellammare and Sorrento, elements of a Roman building were found during the widening of the Autostrada del Sole in 1959 and 1999–2000. Here a series of dining rooms, decorated with fine wall-paintings showing Apollo and the Muses, fronted onto a large courtyard. There was a suite of baths and the complex may have been, or have included, the meeting place of a trades' guild. Wax tablets recovered here in 1959 revealed the business transactions of a local banking family. In another building, 150m further west, skeletons of eight victims were uncovered; one was a woman carrying expensive jewellery including an inscribed snakehead bracelet made of gold. Close by, beside the church of S. Abbondio in the modern town of Pompei, a temple to the god Bacchus, in use from the third century BC onwards, is on view behind railings. The altar in front of the temple was flanked by sets of sloping benches to create an outdoor *triclinium*, where presumably the adherents celebrated the god's feast days. A villa at Scafati belonged to the prominent Lucretii Valentes; in an adjacent graveyard plot, modest headstones were erected over glass urns containing the ashes of the family. Further south-east at S. Antonio Abate, a *villa rustica* discovered in 1974 can be viewed by prior arrangement with the Superintendency of Antiquities.

14. Castellammare di Stabia

Ancient Stabiae, modern Castellammare, long famed for its mineral springs, nestled at the southern end of the Pompeian plain below the Monti Lattari; the 1131m high Monte Faito, reached expensively by cable car from the Castellammare di Stabia train station on the Circumvesuviana line, offers remarkable views on a mist-free day. In antiquity Stabiae served as a seaport for inland Nuceria. Razed in the Social War of 90 BC, the town never recovered its former size. Nevertheless the Bourbon excavations from 1749 onwards revealed an urban area with a rectangular street grid, shops, a temple precinct and baths, which continued to be occupied until AD 79. In 1777 the English traveller Henry Swinburne witnessed some rooms being dug out here. Castellammare is dominated by shipyards, originally established by the Bourbons in 1783 and still functioning. Part of the modern town lies atop volcanic material from the AD 79 eruption, which pushed the coastline forwards.

The escarpment was fringed by Roman villas, partly within the urban area of ancient Stabiae and partly to the south-west of it, overlooking the sea, a setting we have met with at Herculaneum and Pompeii. The ancient shoreline lay a short distance in front. It was at one such villa that the Elder Pliny succumbed to poisonous fumes in AD 79 (above, p. 23). The modern visitor is directed to two villas on the Collina di Varano above the modern town, buried in AD 79 by pumice falls to a depth of less than 3m but not dug out. Discovered originally in the eighteenth century, the villas were re-excavated from 1951 onwards through the initiative of local schoolmaster Libero D'Orsi. From the Circumvesuviana station in Via Nocera, turn left along Via Puglia, then uphill on Via Varano into Via Passeggiata Archeologica. An infrequent bus service, No. 1 Rosso, operates on a circular route past both sites. By car, exit at 'Castellammare di Stabia' on Autostrada A3.

Both villas were built in the late first century BC, with subsequent elaboration, and in the end covered substantial areas. Damaged in the earthquake of AD 62–3, they were still being rebuilt in AD 79. A similar fate awaited them during the 1980 earthquake, after which they remained closed to visitors for many years. Helpful information boards have been donated by

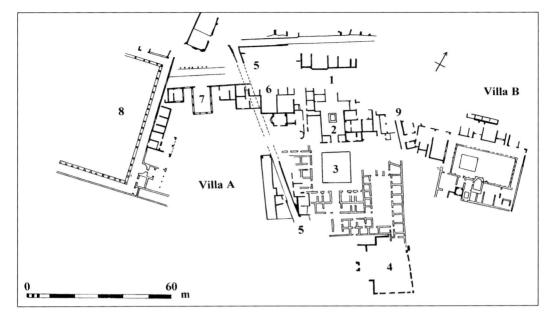

69 Castellammare di Stabia, Villa Arianna: 1. Point of access to visible rooms; 2. *Atrium*;
3. Peristyle; 4. Farm buildings; 5. Access tunnel from beach; 6. *Triclinium*; 7. Summer
dining room; 8. Peristyle; 9. Alley separating Villa A from Villa B. (After Kockel 1985, with
additions)

Rotary International. What seem nowadays two isolated villas were in fact part
of a closely set sequence of luxurious establishments in a choice setting. It is
only when standing on the sites that their marvellous views become evident,
overlooking the curving shoreline back towards Pompeii, and beyond.

The first to be reached from the modern town is the Villa Arianna
(Villa Ariadne), sometimes called the Villa Varano. It lies on Via Passeggiata
Archeologica, access track on the left, which is easily overshot. (Hours: April
– October, 8.30–19.30; November – March, 8.30–17.00. Closed 1 January,
1 May and 25 December.) Rooms of two contiguous villas, 'Arianna A'
and 'Arianna B', separated in Roman times by an alley, form a narrow strip
along the escarpment; the rest is known from the Bourbon site-plan (*69*).
More recently farm buildings – in whose courtyard parts of two wooden
carts were found – were uncovered prior to development. The present-
day visitor arrives at the original nucleus of 'Arianna A', its inland-facing
atrium. To one side was a service wing, and on the other a suite of baths.
A peristyled courtyard was added later, and a series of finely decorated

sea-facing rooms which included two *triclinia*, one with large windows, probably for summer dining in the hottest weather. Consolidation of the friable hillsides continues. A long sloping tunnel led from the beach to the landward side of the villa. Further west was an enormous portico-garden, of which a corner-angle is all that can currently be seen. To the east are some rooms of a separate villa, 'Arianna B'. There was yet another villa lying to the east, the Villa del Pastore, which boasted of a grandiose portico and walkway, baths and possible residential accommodation. This latter complex is thought by some to constitute a health spa of the type found at Baiae.

The visitor should now continue along Via Passeggiata Archeologica, bearing downhill to a track on the left, helpfully signposted for Villa San Marco, which is out of sight beyond its car park. (Hours: April – October 8.30–19.30; November – March 8.30–17.00. Closed 1 January, 1 May and 25 December.)

The layout of the Villa San Marco was constrained by the adjacent urban area of Stabiae, and angled to maximise the view over the Bay (*70*). The visitor enters a modest *atrium* (*71*) containing a *lararium* with a peristyled

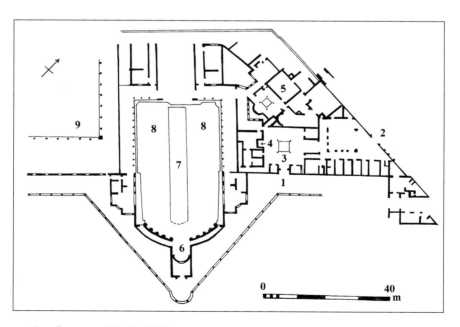

70 Castellammare di Stabia, Villa S. Marco: 1. Entrance; 2. Entrance from Roman town; 3. *Atrium*; 4. *Lararium*; 5. Baths; 6. *Nymphaeum*; 7. Pool; 8. Garden; 9. Peristyle. (After De Vos and De Vos 1982)

garden on the right, where some elements originally exposed in the eighteenth century are being gradually opened up again. Straight ahead were baths whose *caldarium* was heated by a bronze water-tank spirited away by Sir William Hamilton and lost in the wrecking of HMS *Colossus* off the Scillies in 1798. Turning left the visitor reaches a monumental portico with an elongated swimming pool, flanked by lines of plane trees, their roots explored and the species identified by Professor Jashemski. The pool was orientated to face the sea, with a *nymphaeum* at the landward end. Beyond, to the south-west, is part of a second portico on which restoration work continues. A stairway led to lower terraces and to the beach. Fine paintings adorned the rooms, many showing mythological scenes, including Perseus holding aloft the severed head of Medusa, and Iphigeneia, daughter of King Agamemnon. It is easily seen where the Bourbon excavators chiselled out and removed small scenes from the painted walls, which are now at Naples. Tile-stamps found here name Claudius' freedman secretary Narcissus, but whether, as is sometimes supposed, he was the villa's owner or rather the supplier of its roofing tiles, remains unclear. The visitor should now return towards the town by walking downhill, then left on Via Cosenza, to arrive again at the Via Nocera train station.

71 Castellammare di Stabia, reconstructed *atrium* of the Villa S. Marco

An ambitious project, 'Restoring Ancient Stabiae' (www.stabiae.org), led by the University of Maryland, aims to establish an archaeological park, with a study centre and a funicular railway linking the town with the park on the heights above. The town's Antiquarium, long inaccessible to visitors, is scheduled to move to premises in the fourteenth-century Villa Quisisana above the town, after restoration of the latter's dilapidated buildings.

Long ago travellers would take the railway from Naples to its then terminus at Castellammare, where they could expect to find carriages waiting for hire, to carry them to Sorrento (*72*). This is a coastline of high cliffs and narrow inlets, the difficulties of the terrain well seen when the Circumvesuviana train halts at the station for Seiano, perched on a lofty viaduct. The train passes through a sequence of tunnels, while buses and cars

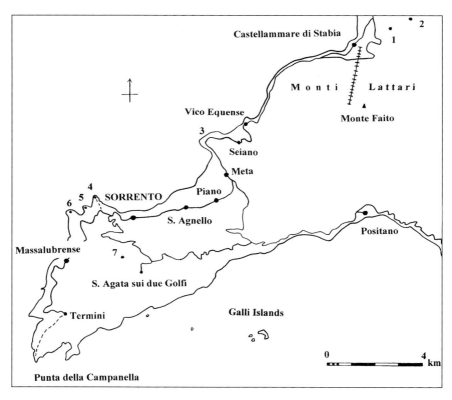

72 Sorrentine Peninsula: 1. Villa Arianna; 2. Villa S. Marco; 3. Punta Scutolo; 4. Capo di Sorrento; 5. Punta della Calcarella; 6. Capo di Massa; 7. Il Deserto

descend the dramatically engineered road past Punta Scutolo, with a view
of the Sorrentine coastline, of cruise ships anchored offshore, and the island
of Capri shimmering in the distance. The coastal cliffs were the home to
several Roman villas, at Marina di Vico, Marina di Equa and at Il Pizzo close
to Marina Ripa di Cassano. At Vico Equense the Antiquarium 'Silio Italico'
in the Palazzo Municipale (at Corso Filangieri, 98) displays Greek vases
dating from the sixth and fifth centuries, from nearby cemeteries.

At Piano di Sorrento the Museo Archeologico della Penisola Sorrentina
'Georges Vallet' at the Villa Fondi overlooking the Bay houses Greek and
Roman material from Vico Equense, Sorrento, Massalubrense and Punta della
Campanella. (Walk downhill from the Circumvesuviana station at Piano to
Via Ripa di Cassano, or proceed on foot from Sant'Agnello.) A *nymphaeum*,
exquisitely decorated with blue and white mosaics of Julio-Claudian date,
from a seaside villa at Marina della Lobra beyond Massalubrense, has been
carefully reconstructed outdoors in the museum's attractive garden.

15. Sorrento

The many holidaymakers who throng the narrow streets of Sorrento
remain, it may be suspected, largely unaware of the town's Roman past,
but archaeological remains do survive in the town, though they are by no
means a conspicuous feature of it.

Roman Surrentum occupied a well defended position at the south-
western end of the plain which lies between it and the village of Meta. The
town was defined both to the west and east by ravines, the more easterly
now partly filled in to create the Piazza Tasso, the present-day main square
(*73*). The modern town did not begin to expand meaningfully eastwards
along the road to S. Agnello until the 1950s.

The area east of Piazza Tasso lay outside the Roman town. Columns
and other architectural fragments, found when the exclusive Grand Hotel
Excelsior Vittoria was built in 1834, are displayed in its gardens, and more
recently the construction of an outdoor swimming pool brought to light
walling in *opus reticulatum*, which is preserved in situ.

Well-preserved cisterns, signposted on Corso Italia near the cinema and
the Standa supermarket, were fed by an aqueduct channel, but they are not
open to visitors. The existence of a bathing complex in Via Correale was
suggested after the discovery there in 1971 of a life-size female statue now at

the museum in Piano. The statue fell over in AD 79, and was buried under pumice.

The Museo Correale di Terranova (Via Correale, 50) was the eighteenth-century country home of a wealthy local family. Among its varied collections are musical instruments, decorative arts and paintings (Hours: 9.00–14.00; closed Tuesdays). An archaeological section on the ground floor displays Roman altars, tombstones, statue bases, sarcophagi, sculptures, inscribed lead water pipes, a sculptured base of Augustan or Tiberian date showing Roman gods and goddesses, and an inscription marking the restoration to working order in AD 80 by Emperor Titus of a water clock damaged by earthquake, presumed to be that of AD 79. Architectural fragments adorn the Museum's peaceful garden, and from its upper floors there are fine views across the Bay to the Roman villa at Capo di Sorrento (see below), further on clear days.

The area known as Sottomonte, between Sorrento and S. Agnello, has yielded numerous simple epitaphs to imperial slaves, the latter presumably

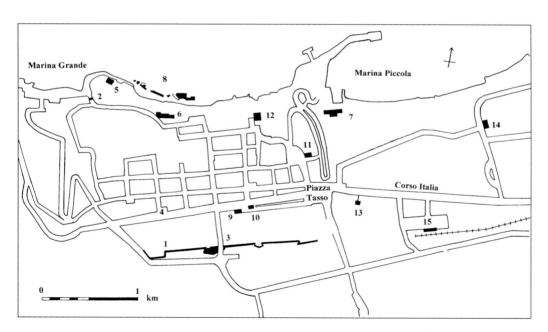

73 Sorrento: 1. Town walls; 2. Marina Grande gate; 3. Parsano Nuova gate; 4. Piazza Veniero; 5. Villa Tritone; 6. Hotel Bellevue Syrene; 7. Grand Hotel Excelsior Vittoria; 8. Offshore structures; 9. Cathedral; 10. Bell-tower; 11. Basilica of S. Antonino; 12. Church and cloister of S. Francesco; 13. Cisterns; 14. Villa Correale; 15. Circumvesuviana train station

employed at an adjacent villa, rather than, as long ago interpreted, marking the burial places of slaves who died on Capri and were shipped back to the mainland. Displayed until recently at the Museo Correale on an outside wall, the small slabs have now been taken down. Other structures along the coastline are overlain by villas of the eighteenth and nineteenth centuries, some long since converted into hotels or religious establishments. A side-chapel in the parish church in Piazza S. Agnello is paved with a marble floor presumably brought from an adjacent villa.

Some elements of the original Graeco-Roman walls of Surrentum are incorporated in much later defences. One of the original gates survives, on the north-west side leading to the Marina Grande. The defensive walls can be followed on the south side of the town, along Via dei Mura Antiche, to the town's south gate which has been excavated beside a medieval successor, the Porta Parsano Nuova. The chequerboard street grid of the Roman town is most obvious in the network of alleys immediately west of Piazza Tasso and north of Corso Italia. The town's Forum has been localised between Corso Italia and Via Fuoro. When Piazza Veniero towards the western end of the Corso was recently landscaped, rooms with painted walls were revealed below it.

Public buildings of the Roman era mentioned by early travellers are conspicuous by their disappearance from view. Three large stone bases are embodied at ground level in the eleventh-century bell-tower adjacent to the cathedral, their inscribed faces hidden from view, though sacrificial implements are visible on the sides of two of them. Column shafts too were re-used there (74) and at the east door of the fifteenth-century cathedral. Architectural fragments and a small inscribed tombstone are preserved within the cathedral, in the first side-chapel on the right. At the Ristorante La Lanterna (Via San Cesareo, 23), on the site of public baths uncovered in 1994, diners at tables indoors can gaze downwards at Roman mosaic floors illuminated through glass-covered inspection pits.

Various churches overlie, or are claimed to overlie, Roman temples. The Basilica of S. Antonino, the sailors' church in the piazza of the same name, sports marble columns taken from Roman buildings. Other columns flank one of its side-doors. Four more are re-used in the cloister of the nearby fourteenth-century monastery of S. Francesco.

Like many of the Roman towns on the Bay, the seafront at Surrentum was given over to the houses of the wealthy. The famous Hotel Bellevue Syrene overlies part of a property traditionally identified as at one time belonging

74 Sorrento, Roman columns re-used in the cathedral bell-tower. (L. Keppie)

to Agrippa Postumus, the grandson of Augustus, whither he was despatched from Rome before his exile to the island of Planasia (near Elba) in AD 8. The Roman villa extended along the cliffs between the Hotel Bellevue Syrene and the Villa Tritone, the latter overlooking the Marina Grande (see p. 12). At the Bellevue Syrene a Roman-style pergola (visible from the public street through a small window on Via Marina Grande) graces its open-air restaurant. In 1906 William Waldorf Astor erected the 'Villa Pompeiana' here, which he modelled on parts of the then recently excavated House of the Vettii at Pompeii with stuccoed ceilings and mosaic floors. An impressively sculpted funerary altar sits in one corner of the restaurant.

Caves in the cliffs at or near sea level, below the hotel, were used for dining, others for breeding fish. Enigmatic stone foundations offshore are clearly visible from above, submerged in the clear waters among the bathing platforms (*colour plate 22*). They could be part of the Roman villa's offshore amenities, but have never been convincingly explained. The novelist James Fenimore Cooper, who in 1829 had rented a nearby house on the cliff-top, observed them from above; he identified them with a Temple of Neptune. Cooper's party regularly utilised the sea-level caves as changing rooms when bathing.

16. From Capo di Sorrento to Punta della Campanella

The modern tourist is unlikely to pay much attention to any sites beyond Sorrento and, when beginning a journey in search of archaeological remains, will naturally travel north-eastwards in the direction of Castellammare and Pompeii. Roman villa-owners of course knew of no such demarcation line, and several of their seaside properties have been detected along the coast, from Sorrento and Massalubrense as far as the tip of the Bay, and round into the Gulf of Salerno. Indeed, between Sorrento and the Punta della Campanella at the southern extremity of the Bay, at least 20 villa-sites are suggested by the survival of structural remains against the cliffs and finds of sculpture.

Though the impressiveness of their visible remains in no way matches sites further north, one villa-site is well worth a visit, not least for its topographical setting. The villa's flat-topped platform is immediately visible from the coastal road at Punta Scutolo (above, p. 151) and from the seafront at Sorrento. Projecting into the Bay the site afforded its owner fine views towards Ischia, Miseno and Naples, the slopes of Vesuvius and the nearer cliff-top towns. All the while speedboats on the adjacent waters hasten across the Bay, and expectant passengers on the numerous hydrofoils and ferries head en masse for Capri, which lies just out of sight, as though summoned to its confined streets by Siren voices, without, it may be supposed, a sideways glance at the site of Roman villa, which is now favoured by a chiefly local clientele for swimming and sunbathing (75). To reach it take a local bus 'A' to its terminus at the former hamlet of Capo di Sorrento. Walk downhill opposite the bar towards the shore on a well-paved but increasingly steep pathway till the sea comes into view. Allow 15 minutes for the descent, longer for the return.

The villa at Capo di Sorrento extended over a substantial area, not just atop the flattened platform itself, but against the steep cliffs behind, where some remnants of the original terracing protrude. It was probably built in the early first century AD, and repaired in the aftermath of the AD 79 eruption. What we see at the site nowadays are mostly cisterns and storage compartments on the lower slopes of the platform, almost totally lacking the stucco-work which once decorated them; what remains has been defaced by modern graffiti. On the summit overgrown foundation walls of rooms face inwards towards a colonnaded court, including a centrally placed *triclinium* on the north side, probably looking out on to a garden with a central fountain. The summit – the remains here elucidated during

75 Capo di Sorrento, villa seen from the sea

consolidation work in 1981 – was later topped by a small medieval chapel to S. Fortunata, now reduced to its foundations, and by a sixteenth-century watchtower (76). The residential wing of the villa, with rooms on several levels, was on the east side, facing Surrentum. In front was a private jetty.

Particularly dramatic is the way in which the villa was crafted by its architect round a natural basin, whose narrow entrance from the sea was dramatically arched over in brick (*colour plate 23*). The basin is known as the Bath of Queen Giovanna (Queen Joan), after an Angevin ruler of Naples in medieval times. There is regrettably no information board or interpretation panel. The appearance of the villa in antiquity is best appreciated by looking at the splendid model of it currently on display in the Museo della Penisola Sorrentina at Piano (above, p. 151).

This villa at Capo di Sorrento was traditionally identified with a property memorably described in detail by the poet Statius in the late first century AD, in a poem dedicated to its then owner, Pollius Felix; hence the site is known in Italian as Villa di Pollio. Statius commends the villa's fine columns, in marbles brought from Greece, Asia Minor, Egypt and Africa; its rooms each had different views to distant landmarks. A steaming bath-house on the beach and a colonnade zigzagging up the cliffs to the villa above were distinguishing features.

Statius' account does not accord well with the setting of the villa at Capo: it is odd that the poet makes no reference to the latter's most distinguishing feature, the inflow of seawater into the central basin. The presence of other villas just to the south, on Punta della Calcarella and on Capo di Massa, allows a more measured assessment. Little survives of the villa currently most favoured as Pollius', on Punta della Calcarella, apart from pavements and some walling. Further to the south, however, at the southern end of the Marina di Puolo (a name which some hold to be a corruption of the Latin Pollius), on the headland of Capo di Massa now marked by a Saracen tower,

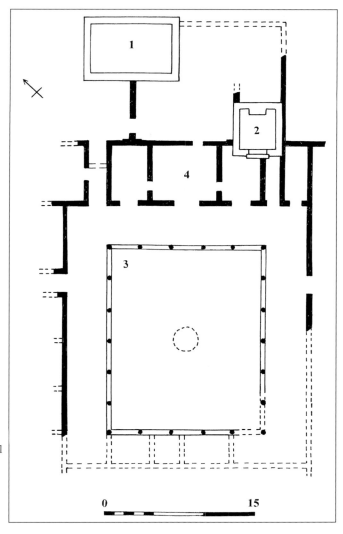

76 Capo di Sorrento, plan of the villa: 1. Medieval tower; 2. Chapel of S. Fortunata; 3. Peristyle; 4. *Triclinium*. (After Russo 2006)

and above a small cove where boats could safely land, extensive remains survive against the cliffs. Starting again from the terminus of Bus 'A' at Capo, walk with care along the busy Sorrento-Massalubrense road, soon turning downhill to follow Via Calata Puolo, a pleasant descent through vineyards to the beachfront at Marina di Puolo. There is access to both ends of the beach by car from the same road, with parking.

The villa here extended widely over the headland, but everything is now heavily overgrown. The Capo di Massa site, with walls in *opus reticulatum* and *opus latericium*, and stairways between levels, originated in the Late Republican or Augustan periods, but with later additions. The site has yielded four marble reliefs of Hadrianic date, now in the museum at Piano, depicting Bacchus, his companions the Satyrs, a sanctuary of Cybele, the Anatolian mother goddess, and a sacrifice to Diana, goddess of hunting. Pollius Felix and his neighbours all enjoyed splendid views across the Bay to Naples, Capo di Miseno, Procida and Ischia on clear days.

From Massalubrense it is a further 5km to the southernmost point on the Bay, the Punta della Campanella. To reach it take a SITA bus from Sorrento to the village of Termini and from the church walk downhill on Via Campanella, then bear right as the signposts direct. A very pleasant and popular walk brings the visitor after 2.5km to the promontory itself. Cars are permitted to a mid point on the road, after which walking is obligatory. The path winds downhill almost to sea level, with Capri all but within shouting distance across the intervening waters. An early start from Termini ensures that both legs of the journey can be traversed on foot mainly in the shade, especially the stiff return climb to the village. The promontory itself is marked by a medieval stone watchtower, one of several closely set along the coast south-west of Sorrento, and by a lighthouse.

The headland was famed in antiquity for its Greek temple dedicated to Athene and later to her Roman equivalent Minerva, and was hence known in antiquity as Cape Athenaion or Promunturium Minervae. The temple was believed to have been founded by Odysseus on his homeward voyage from the Trojan War. The approach road, traditionally called *Via Minervae*, in some places preserves its ancient paving (*77*), with evidence of later repairs and desultory spreads of modern tarmac. The coastline around the Punta della Campanella is now a protected marine area.

Surprisingly there seems no level terrace on which the famous Temple of Athene/Minerva may have stood, though architectural terracottas from its structure and votive offerings left by worshippers were recovered in 1990.

Perhaps it lay on higher ground, unless it was somehow incorporated into or supplanted by a Roman villa which later occupied the terrace where the medieval stone tower now stands. Yet, the temple is depicted as still standing on the medieval Peutinger Table.

The Roman villa, it has been suggested, could have served as a staging post for access to Capri, given that the Villa Jovis (below, p. 161) is in view on a headland opposite. A rock-cut stairway led to a cave at lea level on the western side of the promontory, and an Oscan (native Italic) inscription, datable to the second century BC recording its supervisory magistrates, was spotted, remarkably, on the east side, where steps lead up a natural rock fissure from a landing place. The headland, with its small bays and nearby rocky islands, was one of the locations linked with the Sirens, those female-headed birds who lured sailors to their doom on the rocks below and who had captivated Odysseus and his crew.

77 Punta della Campanella, paving of the *Via Minervae*. (L. Keppie)

In the hills high above Sorrento, the village of S. Agata sui due Golfi (Saint Agatha on the two Gulfs) derives its name from a position affording views not only across the Bay itself but also eastwards into the Gulf of Salerno. Just a short distance from the village is the former monastery of Il Deserto, suppressed in Napoleonic times by the French. From its tower the visitor enjoys a quite spellbinding view across the short intervening distance to the island of Capri, which seems to float magically on the waters, the frequent mists adding to the romantic aura.

Archaeological sites along the coastline towards Amalfi and beyond lie outside the scope of this guidebook, but traces have been found, as might well have been expected, at Positano, Amalfi and Ravello. The visitor to Minori, a little beyond Amalfi, can see remains of a substantial villa with sea-facing gardens; finds are kept in an on-site museum.

17. Capri

The island of Capri dominates the south end of the Bay, like a stately liner moored off the coast, gradually coming into view. Almost certainly once joined to the mainland, from which it is now separated by a strait of some three miles (5km), the island can be reached by ferry or hydrofoil from Sorrento and Naples. The intending visitor is advised to start early, as the island's harbour area and the town squares soon become congested; such is the pressure on the confined streets. The last boats of the day are timed to leave the island by about 20.00. In modern times Capri (ancient Capreae, which means 'hares' or perhaps 'she-goats'), the accent properly on the *first* syllable, has been feted as the one-time home of Norman Douglas, Axel Munthe, Sir Compton Mackenzie, Gracie Fields and Graham Greene, and for the Blue Grotto.

The island was colonised by the Greeks and later it belonged to Neapolis. Under Augustus it passed into imperial ownership, with the Neapolitans receiving Ischia in exchange (above, p. 30). In antiquity, as today, there were two main centres of habitation: Capri town above the Marina Grande, and the more distant Anacapri on higher ground further west (*78*).

Augustus undoubtedly had a villa on Capri. Here he placed on view 'the bones of giants and the weapons of heroes', perhaps found on the island and if so mirrored by the discovery in 1905–06 of fossilised animal bones of the Middle Pleistocene era, in association with Palaeolithic hand-axes

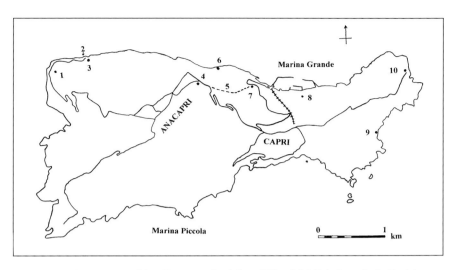

78 Capri: 1. Damecuta; 2. Blue Grotto; 3. Gradola; 4.Villa of S. Michele; 5. Scala Fenicia;
6. Sea Palace; 7. Church of S. Costanzo; 8. Gasto (*villa rustica*, see p. 33); 9. Matromania cave;
10.Villa Jovis

datable to 250,000–150,000 BC, below an extension to the Grand Hotel
Quisisana, deposited there at a time when Capri was not yet separate from
the Sorrentine Peninsula.

Emperor Tiberius, who lived on Capri for most of the final 11 years
of his reign, maintained or established 12 villas on the island, named after
the Olympian Gods, which antiquaries endeavoured to place in favoured
locations. The best known and by far the best preserved is the so-called
Villa Jovis (Villa of Jupiter), at the far north-eastern corner of the island. It
is reached from the main square in Capri town by a walk of 1.5km along a
narrow lane, hemmed in by the perimeter walls of private houses, following
Via Le Botteghe,Via Tiberio and latterly Viale Maiuri, named after the villa's
excavator.

The cliff-top Villa Jovis (a name deduced from Tacitus' *Annals*), set at a
height of 335m (1095ft) above sea level, enjoyed wide views back across
the island to the saddle occupied by Anacapri, and over the narrow strait
towards the adjacent Punta della Campanella. Its many rooms are now
largely bereft of marble cladding, mosaic floors, plasterwork and statuary, all
long since stolen away or removed to churches on the island and Bourbon
palaces on the mainland. The surviving walling chiefly represents water
cisterns and stores on the lowest levels of a very uneven site, which rose to

four or five storeys and was probably topped by gardens, making it difficult to appreciate their former grandeur (*79*). Some of the arcadings in standard reconstructions look strikingly modern.

Constructional techniques, including *opus vittatum mixtum,* which involved interspersing stone facings with bands of horizontal brick coursing (*80*), and *opus latericium,* suggest a number of building phases, perhaps from Tiberius' reign to that of Domitian in the late first century AD.

The villa's residential wing lay to the north. Here a covered passageway led to a promenade, where a grand *triclinium* opened on to the sea, with fine views towards Naples and the far side of the Bay. Grand reception rooms lay to the east, including a magnificent semicircular apse. There was a service wing to the west and a bath complex to the south, catching the sun. The villa is now topped by the medieval Chapel of S. Maria del Soccorso. A solid signal tower, originally accessed along an arched viaduct from the main building, suffered in an earthquake shortly before Tiberius' death in AD 37; presumably it served for communicating with the mainland opposite. A poorly preserved structure to the south-west, traditionally identified as a *specularium*, the observation post in use by Tiberius' favourite astrologer, Thrasyllus, has more recently been suggested as the foundation of a much larger lighthouse, a guide to shipping at the southern end of the Bay.

Though Tiberius' allegedly scandalous pastimes on Capri were emphasised by later historians, this was a cultivated atmosphere of philosophers and scholars. As the aim was for seclusion not public events, it is far from surprising to find no theatre, *odeum* or stadium of the types found at villas elsewhere on the Bay, but we can surely presume there were fountains and extensive gardens. According to the biographer Suetonius, sailors from the naval base at Misenum waited at the foot of the nearby cliffs to finish off victims thrown at Tiberius' command from the summit.

The Cathedral of S. Stefano in Capri town (in Piazza Umberto I) has two *opus sectile* floors from Roman buildings, in front of the great altar and in an adjacent side-chapel. The Centro Caprense 'Ignazio Cerio' (in nearby Piazzetta Ignazio Cerio) displays the Middle Pleistocene fossils found at the Hotel Quisisana, including mammoth, rhinoceros and hippopotamus, and an array of fragments of wall-paintings, mosaics and potsherds collected on the island. Other private collections too preserve remnants of the island's Roman past, among them that formed by the nineteenth-century American Colonel J.C. MacKowen, at the Casa Rossa (Via G. Orlandi, Anacapri).

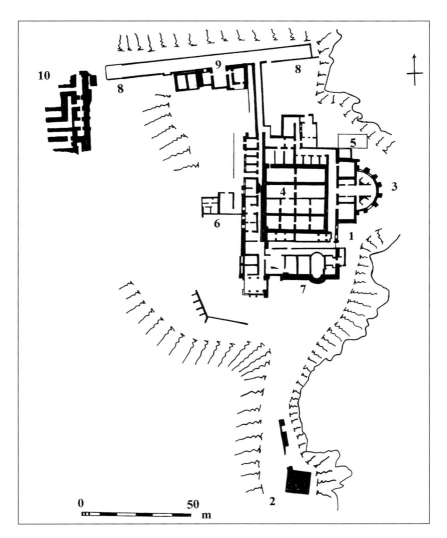

79 Capri, Villa Jovis: 1. Entrance; 2. Lighthouse tower 3. Apsed hall; 4. Cisterns; 5. Chapel of S. Maria del Soccorso; 6. Kitchens; 7. Baths; 8. Promenade; 9. *Triclinium*; 10. *Specularium*. (After Maiuri 1948)

A second Roman villa, the Villa Damecuta, lies at the matching north-west corner of the island (service bus from Anacapri to Grotta Azzurra / Torre Damecuta) near the heliport. Foundations revealed in 1937–48 are laid out for viewing, adjacent to a circular medieval watch-tower. The walling of a once massive apsed structure recalls the east wing of the Villa Jovis, but it is

80 Capri, walling faced in courses of stone and brick (*opus vittatum mixtum*), in the east wing of the Villa Jovis. (James J. Walker)

poorly preserved (*81*). A pleasant covered walk led from it along the cliff-top for a distance of 80m to modest residential accommodation, affording the emperor, it has been suggested, marvellous views across the Bay to Vesuvius, Naples and Miseno. The villa was apparently abandoned after AD 79.

At nearby Gradola, other remnants of indeterminate purpose sit high above the entrance to the Blue Grotto. Here the visitor can watch small boats jockeying for position as they await their turn to enter. That the Blue Grotto was a feature of the island in ancient times too was dramatically demonstrated in 1964 and 1974 when statues of three Tritons and a bearded Neptune were discovered in its waters. Caves elsewhere round the island, including the Grotta di Matromania on the south-east coast, served as shrines or the setting for dinner parties.

Remnants of another Roman villa, occupying the heights of Capo-dimonte overlooking the Marina Grande, are now incorporated into the garden of the Villa of San Michele built by the Swedish doctor Axel Munthe (1857–1949), where he lived intermittently. To reach it take the bus from the harbour or from Capri town to Piazza Vittoria, Anacapri, thereafter along Via Capodimonte and its continuation Via Axel Munthe, flanked by souvenir shops and upmarket boutiques.

The Villa of San Michele, bequeathed by Munthe to the Swedish State and subsequently administered by a charitable foundation, is in some ways the most interesting archaeological site on Capri. Munthe had assembled there – through personal collection on the island and by purchase in salerooms at Naples and Rome – a wide range of sculptures, tombstones and marble flooring. These were tastefully deployed to the owner's specifications and under his supervision, some as freestanding architectural elements, some as decorative features, some serving as plant holders, others set into the glistening white walls, both indoors and outdoors. This created a quite amazing effect, rather close, we could imagine, to the original Roman villas on the island with their gardens, pergolas, courtyards and fountains. There are no explanatory labels, the house being almost exactly as Axel Munthe left it. The visitor can move between three floors, and once outdoors walk along a pleasant covered walkway to the chapel, with stunning views over the harbour and beyond. Near the chapel are some surviving walls of the Roman villa which once stood here, in *opus reticulatum*. One room is reconstructed to roof level, its upper walls displaying an array of inscribed fragments. At the

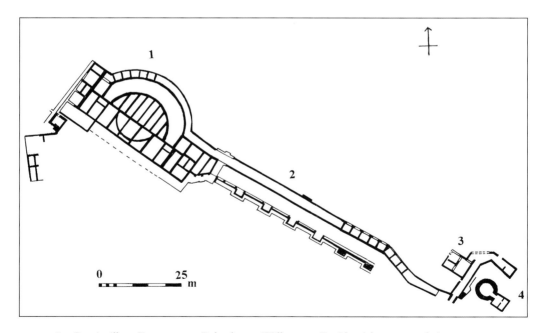

81 Capri, villa at Damecuta: 1. Belvedere; 2. Walkway; 3. Residential accommodation; 4. Medieval tower. (After Maiuri 1948)

far end of the walkway is an Egyptian sphinx in granite from Syene, again purchased at a saleroom. For the intrepid hiker, the Scala Fenicia (Phoenician Staircase) – 800 rock-cut steps belonging to the phase of Greek colonisation of the island – leads dramatically downwards to the Marina Grande.

Columns from one or more Roman villas can be seen in the tenth-century Church of S. Costanzo on Via Marina Grande close to the bottom of the Scala Fenicia. Excavation in 1990–91 showed that the church overlay an Early Christian basilica of the fifth century, itself lying atop a Roman bath-building. Some columns which once graced the church were carried off in 1755 to the Royal Palace at Caserta.

On the shore west of the Marina Grande, and perhaps therefore best visited immediately before re-embarking for the mainland, a further villa, the Sea Palace (Palazzo a Mare), extended along a terrace overlooking the sea. The remains here are disappointingly sparse. However, at the far west end of this complex are the Baths of Tiberius (Bagni di Tiberio) at sea level, where lofty walling in *opus reticulatum* included a semicircular hall, perhaps used for dining. A protected harbour lay in front.

Epilogue

The traveller sailing down the west coast of Italy in Roman times, and approaching the Bay from the north, would have been struck first by the gleaming temple on the acropolis at Cumae, then by the distinctive headland of Capo di Miseno, by oared warships entering and leaving the naval harbours and then, turning east into the Bay with Vesuvius as a perpetual backcloth, soon the steaming rotundas at Baiae and the temple on the promontory at Puteoli above its busy docks and richly ornamented harbour mole. Further east were Neapolis, sloping down towards the sea, Herculaneum on its jutting headland, and Pompeii at the mouth of the Sarno, all the while villas in an almost continuous sequence along the shore or perched on cliff-tops. Then came Stabiae and the plain of Surrentum with the walled town at its western end, with a sequence of high cliffs and narrow gorges. Finally the promontory on which sat the famous temple of Athene/Minerva would come into view, and the sea passage between it and the imperial island of Capri, the latter with numerous villas on its various peaks and headlands.

Travelling Round the Bay:
Advice for the Visitor

Getting There

Naples is accessible directly from many UK airports, especially during the summer months, and by connecting long-haul flights from the US and elsewhere. Naples' Capodichino airport lies immediately west of Vesuvius, so that dramatic views of its crater and of other geographical features described in the foregoing pages may be had on approach or on take-off. For holidaymakers from the UK, a full 'package' is still the norm, though 'flight only' fares are increasingly available. Service buses and a special airport bus take new arrivals from the airport into the city; there is also a direct bus service from the airport to Sorrento and Salerno. Visitors travelling by rail from Rome and heading for Sorrento should change at Napoli Centrale (Piazza Garibaldi) for the lower level station and the Circumvesuviana line, a journey of about 50 minutes on trains designated *direttissimi*; slower trains – which stop at more of the suburban stations – take an extra 15 minutes.

Maps

An excellent 'Kompass' map for walkers at 1:50,000 covers the Bay east of Naples, including the Sorrentine peninsula and the Amalfi coast; a Freytag and Berndt map covers the entire Bay at the same scale. The Touring Club Italiano (TCI) has a map *Golfo di Napoli* at 1:100,000. A large-scale street map of Naples, ideally one with the public transport system marked on it, will prove an essential tool. Succinct guides and site-maps are available free at Pompeii, Herculaneum and Oplontis. Town plans of Sorrento and Pozzuoli will prove useful when seeking out remains there. The images available via 'Live Search' (www.maps.live.com) and 'Google Earth' (www.earth.google.com) can be of value in planning a visit to any site, if the visitor is unsure of its location.

Getting Around

Public transport is cheap and frequent. In recent years there have been numerous initiatives to integrate transport links into a UnicoCampania system, and to encourage tourists to spread their favours beyond the major sites. A rail ticket can now be bought at Sorrento for travel to Pozzuoli (and is valid on buses to Baia and Cuma). Where possible the visitor should obtain a day ticket (*biglietto giornaliero*) for the furthest point on a planned itinerary, which allows intermediate stop-offs and obviates the need to seek out tickets, say in Naples, during the siesta. Single-day 'Weekend' tickets permit a further cost reduction. Tickets should be validated at first use, whether on a bus or at a train station. The network is constantly evolving, always to the traveller's benefit. A new UnicoCostiera ticket allows unlimited travel for 24 hours, with any bus or train company, between Sorrento and the Amalfi coast, and on intermediate routes on the Sorrentine Peninsula. Separate ticketing systems apply on the islands of Capri and Ischia.

The visitor needs always to be on the alert for strikes, but they tend to be of short duration, with written intimation posted on buses and at train stations, usually at least a day in advance. Currently an annual 'summer truce' between the government and unions eases the traveller's anxieties.

The Circumvesuviana railway links Herculaneum, Pompeii and Sorrento with Naples. Some of its stations are attractively named for adjacent archaeological sites (Pompei Scavi Villa dei Misteri, Ercolano Scavi, Torre Annunziata Oplonti Villa di Poppea, Castellammare Ville Romane). The same company operates other lines too, as its name implies, but most visitors are unlikely to need them. Numerous local bus services are also operated by the Circumvesuviana company, but obtaining timetables and routes for them can be difficult; the traveller should consult its website (www.vesuviana.it/reteeorari/ferrovia/larete). The Circumvesuviana's historic 'Too-to-Train' carriages (www.too-to-train.it) offer various excursions, with canapés and refreshments on board, liqueur tasting and other local blandishments. Sales-booths are sited at the principal train stations.

The archaeological sites west of Naples attract fewer visitors. There is no convenient railway to match the Circumvesuviana, but now that the Naples metro

(Linea 2) extends west to Pozzuoli, a visitor can reach the latter from Naples Piazza Garibaldi station in well under an hour and from Sorrento in less than two hours. Several day-trips will be needed to cover the major sites west of Naples. Trains of the Ferrovia Cumana and the Ferrovia Circumflegrea lines, now integrated into the UnicoCampania system, serve the zone west of Naples towards Pozzuoli and Cuma. A limited service by boat (in the summer only) connects Salerno, Sorrento, Naples, Pozzuoli, and Bacoli (www.metrodelmare.com.). The motorway system, especially the Tangenziale to the north and west of Naples, makes access easier by car.

Sorrento is probably the ideal base for visiting the archaeological sites, though certainly not the cheapest; some visitors may prefer to spend time in Naples. An alternative base could be Ischia, beyond the north-west end of the Bay, which is featured by several tour operators, but time needs to be allowed for reaching the mainland at Pozzuoli or Naples before site-visits can begin. The Amalfi coast is too far south to serve as an ideal base for extensive site-visiting by public transport, though of course it is much closer to Salerno and Paestum. Nevertheless the A3 Autostrada westwards from Vietri will bring the visitor by car or coach quickly to Pompeii and Naples.

Site Access and Ticketing

Various types of tickets are available, and can represent a substantial saving if the traveller is able to concentrate visits. A reduced-price ticket for a single visit, in a three-day period, to all five sites in the environs of Vesuvius (Pompeii, Herculaneum, Boscoreale, Oplontis, Castellammare), can be purchased. Another, valid for one day only, covers Oplontis, Castellammare and Boscoreale, for the same price as visiting just one of these three sites. A single ticket, valid for two consecutive days, covers the sites at Baia, Cuma, the amphitheatre at Pozzuoli and the Museo dei Campi Flegrei at Castello di Baia.

The Campania Artecard (www.artecard.com) can be purchased at a number of outlets, for example the major archaeological sites, Naples Archaeological Museum, the airport, Piazza Garibaldi train station, and on-line at www.ticketclic.it. Purchase of an Artecard, valid for three or five days or for a year, covering all Campania, or just parts of it, allows free use of public transport in the designated area (including transport from and to the airport), with free admission to a limited number of major sites of the visitor's choice and substantial discounts at others. A useful booklet, given out with the card, illustrates public transport routes. It is best to buy an Artecard at the airport or on arrival at the first major site or museum being visited, and to begin using it immediately, if full benefit is to be had. The associated Vesuviobus for the Pompeii area and Archeobus for the Campi Flegrei seem regrettably extinct at the time of writing, though still advertised on some websites. The Archeobus was of the greatest value in conveniently linking Pozzuoli with Baia, Miseno and Cuma on a regular basis. However, the recently established 'Retour Campi Flegrei' advertises itineraries by bus westwards from Naples to the main sites and some new attractions (www.retourcampiflegrei.com). The visitor who aims to see all the major sites and museums on the Bay should ideally spend at least a fortnight in the area, with no other major preoccupations.

Free admission to state-owned archaeological sites and museums is accorded to EU citizens under 18 and over 65 years of age. In theory, a passport is needed to confirm identity, but a clear photocopy of it is usually acceptable. Holders of some cultural identity cards may also qualify for free admission. Teachers employed at state schools in the EU can, on production of identification indicating their profession and crucially their country of origin as lying within the EU, have half-price admission. Reduced prices apply too to young persons under 25.

With a few exceptions, the sites described here are either staffed at stated hours, or if unstaffed can be visited at will during daylight, or are visible through railings, or the keyholder's name is posted at the gate. In a few cases, advance notification may be needed by telephone, letter, fax or email, sometimes to the landowner or the nearest available offices of the Superintendency of Antiquities, or a local cultural association. Initiatives promising access are often proposed rather than realised.

The modern visitor to the major sites in high summer needs to arrive equipped for the day ahead, not only with a camera and guidebook, but more importantly with a large bottle of water, a wide-brimmed sunhat and sturdy footwear. Many visitors to Pompeii or Herculaneum, especially those arriving in groups, look ill-prepared for the task ahead.

Opening Hours

The hours given in the text can serve for general guidance only, and are not a guarantee of access at the times stated. Sites, or buildings within them, can be closed for maintenance, repairs or conservation, often at short notice. Opening times may vary according to the seasons of the year. The archaeological sites at Pompeii, Herculaneum, Oplontis, Boscoreale and Stabia have standardised hours (see www.pompeiisites.org), and are closed on only a few days each year. Those west of Naples are also open at standard hours, but some are closed on Mondays. The Archaeological Museum in Naples is closed on a Tuesday. Churches are generally accessible only till midday, then from 16.30 or later, till about 19.30.

Disabled Access

An effort has been made in recent years to make certain museums and some parts of Pompeii accessible to wheelchair users. Details are available on www. turismoaccessibile.it/musei and www.turismoaccessibile.it/monumenti, with information on ramps, lifts and disabled toilets. The generally positive experiences of a wheelchair user and his companion visiting Naples and Capri in 2006 can currently be found on pages entitled 'Navigating Naples' at www. globalaccessnews.com/napleschabner06. Initiatives to cater at Pompeii for the visually impaired visitor have recently been announced.

Safety and Security

Some basic precautions are required. It is ill-advised to stand at a street corner engrossed in a folded-out map, with a bag or camera only loosely attached to one's person. A passport is more secure in a hotel safe than in a pocket. Only cash required for the day should be carried. Stories of street robberies abound, especially in the popular press, and the visitor should take special care at and in the vicinity of the Piazza Garibaldi train station, a focus for pickpockets for well over a century. On the other hand, the author has encountered only friendliness and helpfulness at every turn. Any visitor to Italy will know that standing at a 'zebra crossing' and showing a desire to cross the street will seldom induce traffic to stop in one's favour. The visitor always needs to remember too the effects of heat on his stamina and resolution towards the end of a hot day in high summer.

Glossary

Aedilis	Annually elected magistrate (Aedile), in charge of markets, games and public buildings.
Ambulatio	A walkway or arcade
Apodyterium	The changing room in a bath-building
Architrave	The horizontal course of stonework above the columns of a temple façade, but below the pediment (q.v.)
Atrium	The courtyard beyond the entrance to a house, with a central cistern (*impluvium*, q.v.) in the floor to catch rainwater
Augusteum	Precinct for veneration of Augustus and his family
Augustalis	Freedman member of a guild honouring Augustus and subsequent emperors
Basilica	Colonnaded lawcourt
Bisellium	The double-seat accorded to a magistrate
Caldarium	The hot room in a bath-building
Cardo	A Roman surveyors' term for a north–south street
Castellum aquae	Water-collecting tank
Columbarium	House-shaped collective tomb (lit. dovecote) with numerous niches for the ashes of the deceased
Comitium	Hall where votes were cast in municipal elections
Damnatio memoriae	'Damnation of the memory' of an emperor, his name was erased from inscriptions and whose head removed from statues
Decumanus	A Roman surveyors' term for an east-west street
Decurio	Town councillor, member of the *Ordo decurionum*

Dolium	A bulbous terracotta jar used to store wine or foodstuffs
Duovir	One of the two annually elected chief magistrates of a colony
Forum	The extensive open marketplace at the heart of a town's life
Frigidarium	The Cold Room in a bath-building
Hypocaust	The system of underfloor heating in a bath-building
Impluvium	The cistern in the floor of the *atrium* (q.v.), into which rainwater flowed
Insula	A city-block in a town
Laconicum	The Hot Dry Room in a bath-building
Lapilli	Pumice pebbles ejected from a volcano
Lararium	Household shrine to the *lares*, its protective gods
Macellum	A market building, with shops set round a courtyard
Nymphaeum	A shrine, natural or man-made, with water-features and sculptures of sea nymphs, sometimes used for dining
Odeum	Covered theatre
Opus craticium	Low-cost walling faced in rough stone in a wooden framework.
Opus incertum	Walling where the concrete core was faced with irregularly shaped stones
Opus latericium	Walling where the concrete core was faced with brick
Opus quadratum	Walling in large squared stone blocks
Opus reticulatum	Walling where the concrete core was faced with regularly shaped stones in a diamond pattern
Opus sectile	Flooring of coloured stone or tile, in a geometric pattern
Opus vittatum mixtum	Walling where the concrete core was faced with horizontal brick courses and squared stones
Ordo decurionum	Town Council, up to 100 strong
Oscillum	Sculptured marble disc, often with Dionysiac themes, suspended between columns in a peristyle (q.v.), intended to ward off evil spirits
Palaestra	A large, open exercise yard or sports ground, enclosed by a colonnade
Pediment	The triangular area on the façade of a temple, above

	the architrave (q.v.), which might be filled with sculptures
Peripetal	Term for the free-standing columns along the sides of a temple
Peristyle	A colonnaded courtyard
Pilaster	A squared-off column usually topped by a decorative capital
Pozzolana	Porous volcanic ash quarried near Pozzuoli. When mixed with lime, it set hard on contact with water
Praefurnium	The Furnace Room of a bath-building
Quaestor	One of two annually elected officials in a town, responsible for public finances
Tablinum	The room in a house beyond the *atrium*, used originally to store archives, where the owner stood to receive guests
Telamon	Standing or kneeling figure serving as a masonry support
Tepidarium	The Warm Room in a bath-building
Tesserae	Small cubes of stone, terracotta or glass, which made up mosaic floors
Thermae	A large bathing establishment for public use
Thermopolium	A street-front bar selling food and drink, some of which was stored in the *dolia* (q.v.) set into its counter
Triclinium	The dining room in a house, sometimes outdoors, with three sloping couches for the diners
Tuff	Solidified volcanic stone
Villa maritima	A country house overlooking the sea
Villa rustica	A working farm
Villa suburbana	A country house in proximity to a town

List of Roman Emperors of the First and Second Centuries AD

Augustus (*Imp. Caesar Augustus*)	27 BC–AD 14
Tiberius (*Ti. Caesar Augustus*)	AD 14–37
Gaius Caligula (*C. Caesar Augustus Germanicus*)	AD 37–41
Claudius (*Ti. Claudius Caesar Augustus Germanicus*)	AD 41–54
Nero (*Nero Claudius Caesar Augustus Germanicus*)	AD 54–68
Galba (*Ser. Sulpicius Galba Imp. Caesar Augustus*)	AD 68–69
Otho (*Imp. M. Otho Caesar Augustus*)	AD 69
Vitellius (*A. Vitellius Augustus Imp. Germanicus*)	AD 69
Vespasian (*Imp. Caesar Vespasianus Augustus*)	AD 69–79
Titus (*Imp. Titus Caesar Vespasianus Augustus*)	AD 79–81
Domitian (*Imp. Caesar Domitianus Augustus*)	AD 81–96
Nerva (*Imp. Caesar Nerva Augustus*)	AD 96–98
Trajan (*Imp. Caesar Nerva Traianus Augustus*)	AD 98–117
Hadrian (*Imp. Caesar Traianus Hadrianus Augustus*)	AD 117–38
Antoninus Pius (*Imp. Caesar T. Aelius Hadrianus Antoninus Augustus Pius*)	AD 138–61
Marcus Aurelius (*Imp. Caesar M. Aurelius Antoninus Augustus*)	AD 161–80
Lucius Verus (*Imp. Caesar L. Aurelius Verus Augustus*)	AD 161–69
Commodus (*Imp. Caesar M. Aurelius Antoninus Augustus*)	AD 180–92
Pertinax (*Imp. Caesar P. Helvius Pertinax Augustus*)	AD 193
Didius Julianus (*Imp. Caesar M. Didius Severus Iulianus Augustus*)	AD 193
Severus (*Imp. Caesar L. Septimius Severus Pertinax Augustus*)	AD 193–211

Bibliography

An enormous number of books have been written on individual sites, especially on Pompeii, together with many hundreds of academic papers in learned journals and in conference proceedings, and formal excavation reports. Only a selection can be included here, and I have adopted a chronological sequence, so that the most recent publications appear at the end of each section. The publishing firm Electa Napoli produces a wide range of colourful guidebooks; some of the titles are available in English.

General Guidebooks

Alberti, L. 1550: *Descrittione di Tutta l'Italia* (Bologna)

Sarnelli, P. 1685: *Guida de' forestieri, le cose piu memorabili di Pozzuoli, Baja, Cuma, Miseno* (Napoli)

D'Ancora, G. 1792: *Guida ragionata per le antichità e per le curiosità naturali di Pozzuoli e de' luoghi circonvicini* (Napoli)

Hoare, Sir R.C. 1815: *Hints to Travellers in Italy* (London)

Blewitt, O. 1853: *A Hand-book for Travellers in Southern Italy* (London)

Hare, A. 1883: *Cities of Southern Italy and Sicily* (London)

Forbes, S.R. 1893: *Rambles in Naples, an Archaeological and Historical Guide* (London)

Touring Club Italiano 1927: *Napoli e dintorni* (Milano), and later editions

Francesco, G. (ed.) 1998: *Naples, with Pompeii and the Amalfi Coast* (London/New York), Dorling Kindersley Guide

Blanchard, P. 2000: *Southern Italy* (London), Blue Guide, ed. 7

Nenzel, N.C. 2000: *Ischia, Procida, Capri* (Köln)

Valentino, B. et al. 2007: *Ischia: New Complete Guide* (Casamicciola Terme)

Fuscoe, J. (ed.) 2007: *Naples, Capri, Sorrento and the Amalfi Coast* (London), Time Out Guide

Geography and Geology

Hamilton, Sir W. 1776: *Campi Phlegraei – Observations on the Volcanos of the Two Sicilies* (Naples)

Hamilton, Sir W. 1779: *Supplement to the Campi Phlegraei, being an Account of the great Eruption of Mount Vesuvius in the Month of August 1779* (Naples)

Gunther, R. W.T. 1903: *Contributions to the Study of Earth-movements in the Bay of Naples* (Oxford)

Siggurdsson, H., Cashdollar, S. and Sparks, S.R.J. 1982: 'The eruption of Vesuvius in A.D. 79: reconstruction from historical and volcanological evidence', *American Journal of Archaeology* 86, 39-51

Renna, E. 1992: *Vesuvius Mons* (Napoli)

Pesce, A. and Rolandi, G. 1994: *Vesuvio 1944: l'ultima eruzione* (S. Sebastiano al Vesuvio)

Fröhlich, T. and Jacobelli, L. (eds) 1995: *Archäologie und Seismologie: la regione vesuviana dal 62 al 79 d.C.* (München)

Kilburn, C.R.J. and McGuire, W.J. 2001: *Italian Volcanoes* (Harpenden)

Sørensen, B. 2004: 'Sir William Hamilton's Vesuvian apparatus', *Apollo* 159 (May 2004), 50–57

Conquest and Settlement

Salmon, E.T. 1969: *Roman Colonization under the Republic* (London)

D'Arms, J.H. 1970: *Romans on the Bay of Naples: a social and cultural Study of the Villas and their Owners from 150 B.C. to A.D. 400* (Cambridge, Mass.)

Cornell, T. and Matthews, J. 1982: *Atlas of the Roman World* (Oxford/New York)

Frederiksen M.W. 1984: *Campania* (Rome), ed. N. Purcell

Life and Death

Casson, L. 1974: *Travel in the Ancient World* (London)

Castrén, P. 1975: *Ordo Populusque Pompeianus: Polity and Society in Roman Pompeii* (Roma)

Clarke, J.R. 1991: *The Houses of Roman Italy, 100 AD–AD 250* (Berkeley/Oxford)

Yegül, F.K. 1992: *Baths and Bathing in Classical Antiquity* (New York/London)

Laurence, R. 1994: *Roman Pompeii: Space and Society* (London)

Wallace-Hadrill, A. 1994: *Houses and Society in Pompeii and Herculaneum* (Princeton)

Beard, M., North, J. and Price, S. 1998: *Religions of Rome* (Cambridge)

Zanker. P. 1998: *Pompeii, Public and Private Life* (Cambridge, Mass./London)

Fagan, G. 1999: *Bathing in Public in the Roman World* (Ann Arbor)

Franklin, J.L. 2001: *Pompeis difficile est: Studies in the political Life of Imperial Pompeii* (Ann Arbor)

Carroll, M. 2006: *Spirits of the Dead, Roman funerary Commemoration in Western Europe* (Oxford)

Jones, D.F. 2006: *The Bankers of Puteoli: Finance, Trade and Industry in the Roman World* (Stroud)

Sear, F. 2006: *Roman Theatres, an Architectural Study* (Oxford/New York)

Welch, K. E. 2007: *The Roman Amphitheatre* (Cambridge)

Coastal and other Villas

Carrington, R.C. 1931:'Studies in the Campanian "villae rusticae"', *Journal of Roman Studies* 21, 110–130

McKay, A.G. 1975: *Houses, Villas and Palaces in the Roman World* (London)

Jolivet, V. 1987:'Xerxes togatus: Lucullus en Campagne', *Melanges d'Ecole française de Rome, Antiquité* 99, 875–904

MacDougall, E.B. (ed.) 1987: *Ancient Roman Villa Gardens* (Washington)

Higginbotham, J.A. 1997: *Piscinae – Artificial Fishponds in Roman Italy* (Chapel Hill)

Lafon, X. 2001: *Villa Maritima: recherches sur les villas littorales de l'Italie romaine* (Rome)

Adams, G.W. 2006: *The Suburban Villas of Campania and their Social Function* (Oxford, BAR int. ser. 1542)

Marzano, A. 2007: *Roman Villas in Central Italy* (Leiden)

Archaeology and Dating

Ling, R. 1991: *Roman Painting* (Cambridge)

Adam, J.-P. 1994: *Roman Building: Materials and Techniques* (London)

Descoeudres, J.-P. 1994: *Pompeii revisited: the Life and Death of a Roman Town* (Sydney)

Berry, J. (ed.) 1998: *Unpeeling Pompeii* (Milano)

Ling, R. 1998: *Ancient Mosaics* (London)

DeLaine, J. and Johnston, D.E. (eds) 1999: *Roman Baths and Bathing*, JRA Suppl. no. 37 (Portsmouth, R.I.)

Dunbabin, K.M.D. 1999: *Mosaics of the Greek and Roman World* (Cambridge)

Allison, P. M. 2004: *Pompeian Households, an Analysis of the Material Culture* (Los Angeles)

Travellers, Travelogues and Memoirs

General

Pine-Coffin, R.S. 1974: *Bibliography of British and American Travel in Italy to 1860* (Firenze)

Brigante, G., Spinosa, N., Stainton, L. 1990: *In the Shadow of Vesuvius: Views of Naples from Baroque to Romanticism, 1631–1830* (Naples)

Brendon, P. 1991: *Thomas Cook – 150 Years of Popular Tourism* (London)

Ingamells, J. 1997: *A Dictionary of British and Irish Travellers in Italy, 1701–1800* (New Haven, Conn./London)

Tuck-Scala, A., Plamondon, A.L., Vacca, A. (eds) 2000: *Sorrento: Visiting Paradise, a Literary Guidebook* (Sorrento)

Sixteenth Century

Moryson, F. 1617: *An Itinerary containing his ten Yeeres Travell* (London)

Hoby, T. 1902: *A Book of the Travaille and Lief of me, Thomas Hoby* (London), Camden Miscellany vol. 10

Seventeenth Century

Sandys, G. 1670: *Sandys Travels, containing an History and present State of the Turkish Empire, … Greece… Aegypt … the Holy-Land. Lastly, Italy described* (London)

Lassels, R. 1670: *Voyage of Italy, or a compleat Journey … with Instructions concerning Travel* (Paris/London)

Eighteenth Century

Addison, J. 1705: *Remarks on several Parts of Italy in the Years 1701, 1702, 1703* (London)

Swinburne, H. 1785: *Travels in the Two Sicilies* (London)

Piozzi, H.L. 1789: *Observations and Reflections made in the Course of a Journey through France, Italy and Germany* (Dublin)

Starke, M. 1815: *Letters from Italy* (London)

Goethe, J.W. von 1816–17: *Italiänische Reise* (Weimar), translated by W.H. Auden and E. Mayer as *Italian Journey* (London, 1962)

Hoare, Sir R.C. 1819: *A Classical Tour through Italy and Sicily* (London)

Lewis, W.S. (ed.) 1948: *Horace Walpole's Correspondence*, vols 13–14 (London/New Haven)

Jenkins, I. and Sloan, K. 1996: *Vases and Volcanoes: Sir William Hamilton and his Collection* (London)

Wilton, A. and Bignamini, I. (eds) 1996: *Grand Tour: the Lure of Italy in the Eighteenth Century* (London)

Savelsberg, W. and Quilitzsch, U. (eds) 2005: *Infinitely beautiful: the Garden Realm of Dessau-Wörlitz* (Berlin)

Nineteenth Century

Coxe, Henry 1815: *Picture of Italy, being a Guide to the Antiquities and Curiosities of that classical and interesting Country* (London)

Anon. 1838: *Notes on Naples and its Environs* (London)

Cooper, J. Fenimore 1838: *Excursions in Italy* (London)

Blessington, Lady M. 1839: *The Idler in Italy* (Paris)

Cox, J. 1841: *Hints for Invalids about to visit Naples, being a Sketch of the medical Topography of that City ... also an Account of the Mineral Waters of the Bay* (London)

Dickens, C. 1846: *Pictures from Italy* (London)

Twain, M. 1869: *The Innocents Abroad* (Hartford, Conn.)

Neville-Rolfe, E. (ed.) 1889: *One Day in the Naples Museum, According to the New Arrangement* (Napoli)

Crawford, F. M. 1894: 'Coasting by Sorrento and Amalfi', *The Century Magazine* 26, 325–36

Smith, J. 1899: *A Pilgrimage to Italy* (Aberdeen)

McMahan, A.B. 1907: *With Shelley in Italy* (London)

Gell, Sir W. 1957: *Reminiscences of Sir Walter Scott's Residence in Italy, 1832* (London), ed. J.C. Corson

Clay, E. (ed.) 1965: *Ramage in South Italy* (London)

Clay, E. (ed.), with Frederiksen, M. 1976: *Sir William Gell in Italy* (London)

Powell, C. 1987: *Turner in the South: Rome, Naples, Florence* (New Haven/London)

Twentieth Century

Douglas, N. 1911: *Siren Land* (London)

Hutton, E. 1958: *Naples and Campania revisited* (London)

Trevelyan, R. 1976: *The Shadow of Vesuvius* (London)

Lewis, N. 1978: *Naples '44* (London)

Pitt-Kethley, F. 1988: *Journeys to the Underworld* (London)

Ross, A. 1999: *Reflections on Blue Water* (London)

The Archaeological Sites on the Bay

Guidebooks are marked with an asterisk (*)

General

Beloch, J. 1890: *Campanien: Geschichte und Topographie des antiken Neapel und seiner Umgebung* (Breslau), ed. 2

Grant, M. 1971: *Cities of Vesuvius* (London/New York)

McKay, A.G. 1972: *Ancient Campania* (Hamilton, Ont.)

Jashemski, W. 1979: *The Gardens of Pompeii, Herculaneum and the Villas destroyed by Vesuvius* (New Rochelle)

* Bisi Ingrassia, A.M. 1981: *Napoli e dintorni, guida alla città greco-romana e al suo circondario* (Roma)

* De Caro, S. and Greco, A. 1981: *Campania* (Roma/Bari), Laterza Archaeological Guide

* De Vos, A. and De Vos, M. 1982: *Pompei, Ercolano, Stabia* (Roma/Bari), Laterza Archaeological Guide

Kockel, V. 1985–86: 'Archäologische Funde und Forschungen in den Vesuvstädten', *Arch. Anzeiger* 1985, 495–571; ibid. 1986, 443–60

Parslow, C.C. 1995: *Rediscovering Antiquity: Karl Weber and the Excavation of Herculaneum, Pompeii and Stabiae* (Cambridge)

Guzzo, P.G. (ed.) 2003: *Tales from an Eruption: Pompeii, Herculaneum, Oplontis* (Milano)

Pappalardo, U. 2006: *The Gulf of Naples, Archaeology and History of an Ancient Land* (Verona), translated from *Il Golfo di Napoli* (Verona)

* Pesando, F. and Guidobaldi, M.P. (eds) 2006: *Pompei, Oplontis, Ercolano, Stabiae* (Roma/Bari), Laterza Archaeological Guide

* Touring Club Italiano 2006: *Campania Antica* (Milano)

Gardner Coates, V.C. and Seydl, J.L. 2007: *Antiquity recovered: the Legacy of Pompeii and Herculaneum* (Los Angeles)

Baia

Borriello, M.R. and D'Ambrosio, A. 1979: *Baiae-Misenum* (Firenze), Forma Italiae, i.14

Sciarelli, G.T. (ed.) 1983: *Baia: il ninfeo imperiale sommerso di Punta Epitaffio* (Napoli)

Yegül, F. 1996: 'The thermo-mineral complex at Baiae and the *De Balneis Puteolanis*', *Art Bulletin* 78, 137–61

Miniero, P. 2003: *Baia, the Castle, Museum and Archaeological Sites* (Naples)

Boscoreale

Baratte, F. 1986: *Le trésor d'orfèvrerie romaine de Boscoreale* (Paris)

Anderson, M.L. 1987: *Pompeian Frescoes in the Metropolitan Museum of Art* (New York)

De Caro, S. 1994: *La villa rustica in località Villa Regina a Boscoreale* (Roma)

Capri

Munthe, A. 1929: *The Story of San Michele* (London)

* Maiuri, A. 1948: *Capri, its History and its Monuments* (Rome), and later editions

Federico, E. and Miranda, E. 1998: *Capri antica dalla preistoria alla fine dell'età romana* (Capri)

Freccero, A. 2003: *Roman Marbles, the Art Collection of Axel Munthe* (Capri)

Krause, C. 2003: *Villa Jovis, die Residenz des Tiberius auf Capri* (Mainz)

Castellammare di Stabia

Barbet, A. and Miniero, P. 1999: *La Villa San Marco a Stabia* (Napoli/Roma/Pompei)

Anon. 2000: *La riscoperta di Stabia, l'avventura archeologica di Libero D'Orsi* (Castellammare)

* Bonifacio, G. and Sodo, A.M. 2001: *Stabiae: guida archeologica alle ville* (Castellammare)

Pesce, A. (ed.) 2004: *In Stabiano: Exploring the ancient seaside Villas of the Roman Elite* (Washington)

Magalhaes, M. M. 2006: *Stabiae romana: la prosopografia e la documentazione epigrafica* (Castellammare)

Cuma

Paget, R.F. 1968: 'The Ancient Ports of Cumae', *Journal of Roman Studies* 58, 152–69

Pagano, M. 1986: 'Una nuova interpretazione del cosidetto "Antro della Sibilla" a Cuma', *Puteoli* 9–10 (1985–86), 83–120

* Caputo, P., Morichi, R., Paone, R., Rispoli, P. 1996: *Cuma e il suo Parco Archeologico* (Roma)

Herculaneum

Bayardi, O.A. and Carcani, P. 1757–71: *Le antichità di Ercolano esposte* (Napoli)

* Maiuri, A. 1933: *Herculaneum* (Roma), and later editions

De Seta, C., Di Mauro, L., Perone, M. 1980: *Ville Vesuviane* (Milano)

Guadagno, G. 1983: 'Herculanensium Augustalium aedes', *Chronache Ercolanesi* 13, 159–73

Deiss, J.J. 1985: *Herculaneum, Italy's buried Treasure* (London), ed. 2

Scatozza-Höricht, L.A. 1985: 'Ville nel territorio ercolanese', *Chronache Ercolanesi* 15, 131–65

Belloli, A.P.A. (ed.) 1988: *The J. Paul Getty Museum: Guide to the Villa and its Garden* (Malibu)

Pagano, M. and Balasco, A. 2000: *The ancient Theatre of Herculaneum* (Napoli)

Capasso, L. 2001: *I fuggiaschi di Ercolano: paleobiologia delle vittime dell'eruzione vesuviana del 79 d.C.* (Roma)

Wallace-Hadrill, A. et al. 2005: *Conservation and Management of Archaeological Sites*, vol. 8.4

Mattusch, C.C. 2005: *The Villa dei Papiri at Herculaneum: Life and Afterlife of a Sculpture Collection* (Los Angeles)

Sider, D. 2005: *The Library of the Villa dei Papiri at Herculaneum* (Los Angeles)

* Guidobaldi, M.P. 2006: *Ercolano, guida agli scavi* (Napoli)

Ischia

Monti, P. 1980: *Ischia – Archeologia e Storia* (Napoli)

Buchner, G. and Gialanella, C. 1994: *Museo archeologico di Pithecusae, isola d'Ischia* (Roma)

Miseno

Borriello, M.R. and D'Ambrosio, A. 1979: *Baiae-Misenum* (Firenze), Forma Italiae i.14

Miniero, P. 2000: *The* Sacellum *of the* Augustales *at* Miseno (Napoli)

Naples

Macchiaroli, G. (ed.) 1985: *Napoli Antica* (Napoli), exhibition catalogue

De Caro, S. 1994: *Il museo archeologico di Napoli* (Napoli)

Zevi, F. (ed.) 1994: *Neapolis* (Napoli)

Giampaola, D. and Longobardo, F. (eds) 2000: *Napoli Greca e Romana* (Napoli)

Arthur, P. 2002: *Naples, from Roman Town to City-state, an Archaeological Perspective* (London)

Oplontis

Fergola, L. (ed.) 2004: *Oplontis e le sue Ville* (Pompei)

Phlegraean Fields

* Maiuri, A. 1947: *The Phlegraean Fields, from Virgil's Tomb to the Grotto of the Cumaean Sibyl* (Rome), and later editions

Pagano, M., Reddé, M., Roddaz, J.-M. 1982: 'Recherches archéologiques et historiques sur la zone du Lac d'Averne', *Melanges d'Ecole française de Rome, Antiquité* 94, 271–323

Pagano, M. 1984: 'Il Lago Lucrino, ricerche storiche e archeologiche,' *Puteoli* 7–8 (1983–84), 113–226

Amalfitano, P., Camodeca, G. and Medri, P. (eds) 1990: *I Campi Flegrei, un itinerario archeologico* (Venezia)

De Caro, S. 2002: *I Campi Flegrei, Ischia, Vivara: storia e archeologia* (Napoli)

Gialanella, C. (ed.) 2003: *Nova Antiqua Phlegrea: new archaeological Treasures from the Phlegraean Fields* (Napoli)

Pompeii

Gell, Sir W. and Gandy, J.P. 1817: *Pompeiana: the Topography, Edifices and Ornaments of Pompeii* (London)

* Fiorelli, G. 1875: *Descrizione di Pompeii* (Napoli), reprinted 2001

* Morano, A. 1896: *Guide of Pompeii* (Naples)

* Maiuri, A. 1934: *Pompeii* (Roma), and later editions

Ward-Perkins, J. B. and Claridge, A. 1976: *Pompeii, AD 79* (Bristol)

Connolly, P. 1979: *Pompeii* (London)

D'Ambrosio, A. and De Caro, S. 1983: *Un impegno per Pompei. Fotopiano e documentazione della necropolis di Porta Nocera* (Milano)

Kockel, V. 1983: *Die Grabbauten vor dem Herkulaner Tor in Pompeji* (Mainz)

Franchi dell'Orto, L. and Varone, A. (eds) 1990: *Rediscovering Pompeii* (Roma), exhibition catalogue

Etienne, R. 1992: *Pompeii: the Day a City died* (London)

* La Rocca, E., De Vos, M. and De Vos, A. 1994: *Guida archeologica di Pompei* (Verona), ed. F. Coarelli, new ed.

Borriello, M., D'Ambrosio, A., De Caro, S. and Guzzo, P. G. 1996: *Pompei, abitare sotto il Vesuvio* (Ferrara), exhibition catalogue

Ling, R. et al. 1997–2006: *The Insula of the Menander at Pompeii* (Oxford), 4 vols.

* Nappo, S. 1998: *Pompeii, Guide to the lost City* (London)

Ciarallo, A. and De Carolis, E. 1999: *Homo Faber: natura, scienza e tecnica nell' antica Pompei* (Napoli), exhibition catalogue

De Simone, A. and Nappo, S.C. (eds) 2000: *Mitis Sarni Opes: nuova indagine archeologica in località Moregine* (Napoli)

Jashemski, W. and Meyer, F. G. (eds) 2002: *The Natural History of Pompeii* (Cambridge/ New York)

Coarelli, F. (ed.) 2002: *Pompeii* (New York)

Cooley, A.E. 2003: *Pompeii* (London)

Wilkinson, P. 2003: *Pompeii – The Last Day* (London)

Cooley, A.E. and Cooley, M. G. L. 2004: *Pompeii – a Sourcebook* (London/New York)

Ussani, V. S. (ed.) 2005: *Moregine, suburbio 'portuale' di Pompei* (Napoli)

Ling, R. 2005: *Pompeii, History, Life and Afterlife* (Stroud)

Butterworth, A. and Laurence, R. 2006: *Pompeii – The Living City* (London)

Berry, J. 2007: *The Complete Pompeii* (London)

Dobbins, J.J. and Foss, P.W. (eds) 2007: *The World of Pompeii* (London/New York)

Harris, J. 2007: *Pompeii awakened, a Story of Rediscovery* (London/New York)

Beard, M. 2008: *Pompeii, the Life of a Roman Town* (London)

Posillipo

Alvino, F. 1845: *La Collina di Posilipo* (Naples)

Gunther, R.W.T. 1913: *Pausilypon, the imperial Villa near Naples* (Oxford)

Pozzuoli

Dubois, C. 1907: *Pouzzoles Antique* (Paris)

Anon. 1977: *I Campi Flegrei nell'archeologia e nella storia*, Atti Convegni Lincei 33 (Roma)

Sommella, P. 1978: *Forma e urbanistica di Pozzuoli romana = Puteoli, studi di storia antica 2* (Napoli)

Ostrow, S.E. 1979: 'The topography of Puteoli and Baiae on the eight glass flasks', *Puteoli* 3, 77–140

Purcell, N. 1984: 'Puteoli', in M.W. Frederiksen, *Campania* (Rome), 319–58

Zevi, F. (ed.) 1993: *Puteoli* (Napoli)

De Caro, S., Gialanella, C., Jodice, M. 2002: *Il Rione Terra di Pozzuoli* (Napoli)

Crimaco, L., Gialanella, C., F. Zevi (eds) 2003: *Da Puteoli a Pozzuoli: scavi e ricerche sulla rocca del Rione Terra* (Napoli)

Sorrento

Mingazzini, P. and Pfister, F. 1946: *Surrentum* (Roma), Forum Italiae i.2

Russo, M. 1999: 'Sorrento, edifici pubblici, case private, tabernae', in F. Senatore (ed.), *Pompei, il Vesuvio e la penisola sorrentina* (Roma), 145–231

* Tippett, J, 2000: *Landscapes of Sorrento and the Amalfi Coast: a countryside Guide* (London), ed. 2

Magalhaes, M.M. 2003: *Storia, istituzioni e prosopografia di Surrentum romana* (Castellammare)

Russo, M. 2006: *La villa romana del Capo di Sorrento* (Sorrento)

Index

Numerals in **bold** refer to illustrations